CW00734389

Pondering the Mystery of Life

by

AUDREY C. SHIELDS

For My Cherished Family

Contents

Introduction

Over millennia, spiritual leaders and philosophers have devoted their lives to developing worldviews that could help us achieve enlightened and happier lives. While religious worldviews are most frequently inculcated in childhood, other secular or spiritual viewpoints can be developed as we mature and question "the meaning of life." This study, while hardly exhaustive, will explore a variety of spiritual experiences, including those of a religious nature, that human beings have found meaningful. It includes the speculations of some of our deepest thinkers.

One of the most significant questions we struggle with as human beings is, Does God exist? Is it reasonable to believe or to not believe in the existence of a Creator? The existence of a Divine Being is not provable as an objective truth. We have rational inquiry (philosophy) and we have faith, but neither would satisfy scientific scrutiny. On what evidence and experience do individuals rely in deciding how to respond to the mystery of our existence?

A corollary question that we ask ourselves is, Who or what is God? What concept of Divinity do I believe in or perhaps reject? "God" means different things to different people; thus, the question—Do I believe in God?—needs qualifying. Do I believe in a personal God or any other supernatural Force?

Some of the faithful, known as Fundamentalists, believe in an anthropomorphic God. Fundamentalists rely on a literal interpretation of their sacred texts and/or believe they were inspired by God. Other believers, sometimes referred to as Progressives, interpret the same sacred texts metaphorically or symbolically, as stories or myths told by enlightened writers to explain the workings of the universe and mankind's role in it. Nonetheless, Progressives believe in an Ultimate Reality, which they call "God."

A growing number of Americans and Western Europeans, sometimes called "nones," or non-affiliated, have abandoned religion. While they are not unanimous in rejecting some "higher power," nearly thirty percent of adult Americans "describe themselves as athe-ists, agnostics, or 'nothing in particular' when asked about their religious identity."[1] Among the nonreligious there are many who turn to alternative, secular paths for spiritual growth.

Our questions and answers are, of course, nothing new. They have roots in the ancient past, as well as in more recent centuries, often giving rise to religious belief, which can be consoling in a troubled world, and experience tells us that material goods alone are insufficient for our happiness. We wonder if there isn't something more substantial on which we can rely for well-being.

It is quite amazing how varied are people's responses to the challenge of understanding life. Researchers have counted thousands of religions. The one thing apparently ubiquitous is the need to make some sense of life. The mystery of the universe may be eternal, but thinking people will continue to search for meaning and try to live accordingly. Let us keep open minds and hearts while exploring some of the ways that one can respond to the challenge.

---

[1] "About Three-in-Ten U.S. Adults Are Now Religiously Unaffiliated," *pewforum.org* (December 14, 2021).

Literal Belief

In each of the monotheistic religions there are those who claim certitude in their belief in the existence of God because they subscribe to the literal truth of their sacred texts.

For example, traditional Christians cite the biblical account of Christ's Resurrection as proof that there is a God. Resurrection from the dead would, of course, involve a supernatural intervention.

Traditional Muslims, who comprise nearly ninety percent of all Muslims, believe that the stories and moral guidance contained in their sacred text, the Koran, were revealed by Allah to the Prophet Mohammed in visions.

Mohammed is believed to have been visited by the archangel Gabriel in a cave in 600 CE.

Mormons, too, base their belief in God on revelation, specifically on a series of visions experienced by one Joseph Smith in nineteenth century America. Again there is no objective evidence, unless one believes, as Mormons do, that an angel directed Joseph to the location of buried golden plates that he ultimately translated into the Book of Mormon before returning them, as he said, to the angel.

Judaism became a monotheistic religion about 4000 years ago through the Prophet Abraham, the patriarch of Judaism. Many ultra-orthodox Jews believe that Abraham had frequent conversations with God and that God appeared to him. They believe that some centuries later the Torah, comprising the first five books of the Old Testament, was dictated to Moses by God on Mount Sinai and that it has been preserved without error for three millennia.[2] It includes the story of the Creation, as well as that of Adam and Eve.

Nonbelievers and even some believers in God do not accept the literal truth of such miracles. Certain twenty-first century atheists known as "New Atheists" have taken issue with the supernatural nature of such Fundamentalist claims. Richard Dawkins, an evolutionary biologist, for example, has protested against the central tenet of Christianity, the Resurrection of Jesus Christ, suggesting that the four versions of the Resurrection in the gospels contradict one another.[3] A further observation is that in the myths of the ancient world, supernatural events such as rising from the dead and virgin births are not all that rare, even commonplace.[4]

As to the cause of dreams and consciousness, Dawkins suggests that it is possible that our brains have not yet sufficiently evolved to understand their cause. While scientists continue to research the origin of dreams and visions, our uncertainty, these thinkers proclaim, is not a reason to give them a supernatural origin.

[2] Marc Zvi Brettler, "Did God Write the Torah—and Does it Matter?" *myjewishlearning.com.*

[3] "Richard Dawkins and Lawrence Krauss, "How the Universe Came from Nothing," YouTube.

[4] Joseph Campbell, "Masks of Eternity," *Joseph Campbell and the Power of Myth*, Ep. 6, *billmoyers.com* (June 26, 1988).

Progressive (Non-literal) Ways of Defining God

Many believers are not insistent on the literal truth or the directly inspired nature of the Scriptures. They believe in Divinity, but they believe we can speak of "God" only metaphorically. Some of the ways in which they define God, for example, are the following: God is beauty; God is a force; God is "the ground of being"; God is "the primary thing"; God is "immaterial essence"; and God is "the being greater than which none can be conceived."[5]

One of the most important theologians of the twentieth century, the American Protestant Reinhold Niebuhr, wrote, for example, that he believed in a transcendent God who, he says, is "at once the creator of the world (source of its meaning) and judge of the world (that is, goal of its perfection.)"[6] In other words, Niebuhr extends the anthropomorphic interpretation of "creator" and "judge" to the more metaphorical "source of existence" and "reason for being."

While his theology is called Christian Realism, Niebuhr worked within the movement that is known as "neo-orthodoxy," insisting on the mysterious nature of God and on a non-literal interpretation of the Bible. He was, nonetheless, a person of faith. "Theology is … a rational explication of man's faith," Niebuhr once told an interviewer.[7] Faith undergirds reason.

Another American Protestant who turns to Scripture both in her life and in her work is the prize-winning American novelist Marilynne Robinson (*Gilead*). Her reading of the Bible is likewise non-literal. Concerning God, Robinson has said it is "a widespread intuition" that there is "a profound Intelligence behind everything."[8]

God's character, she says, can be conceived by way of intuition, as well as by considering human morality. Her thinking is akin to the reasoning of the German philosopher Immanuel Kant (1724-1804). Kant believed that we are designed to have intuitions, that it is natural for human beings "to have ideas that exceed . . . the grasp of their minds." He argued that we have built-in (*a-priori*) structures that allow us to form concepts of reality. We can intuit a transcendent reality that we call God.[9] Contemporary philosophers warn, however, that "intuition lacks the clarity and comprehensiveness" of conceptual thinking. It can be "a starting point for further deliberation ... but it can also be misleading in that it conjures up a sense of finality."[10] Believers like Robinson are aware of the limitations of intuition, but find it an important ingredient in the framework of their religious faith.

Kant believed, too, that we can attribute qualities to that Supreme Reality by looking at

His creation, particularly mankind. Our moral sense, which each of us has by virtue of being human, is proof of God's unconditional goodness. It is immanent and it moves us towards the Divine.[11] Robinson and Niebuhr would agree; moreover, Niebuhr wrote, "the highest human excellencies are clues to the character of God."[12] God is caring; God is just; God is merciful.

Regarding the apprehension of what is real through intuition, Romantic poets like William Wordsworth and William Blake believed that feelings are true and that, along with imagination, they can help us to apprehend the whole of reality. Blake could "see a World in a grain of sand / And a Heaven in a Wild Flower."[13] They were referring to subjective "truth."

Intuitions are based on the emotions that arise from one's subconscious; however, they can be tested by rational thought.[14] The proposition that instinct and imagination could lead to a kind of knowledge was of great significance to the philosophers Charles Sanders Peirce and William James who established the influential philosophical tradition known as Pragmatism. Pragmatism implies faith in common sense and in instinct. Peirce believed that "our instinctive sentiments may guide us correctly."[15]

Peirce, a scientist, saw prayer as an impulse that rises instinctively and naturally as a response to our world. Prayer, he felt, is "the place to which thought retreats when it cannot make progress."[16] Pragmatism suggests that religious experience in general is useful in that "it connects us with a greater, or further, reality not accessible to our normal cognitive relations to the world." Moreover, it is good for the body and "soul."

Peirce's fellow Pragmatist William James, a renowned philosopher, psychologist, and Harvard professor, taught likewise that "one of the pragmatic benefits of belief is a more reliable access to reality."[17] In a famous lecture entitled "The Will to Believe," James defends belief even when the evidence to prove the hypothesis is missing. If you want to pursue inquiry into a truth, he points out, you must first entertain the possibility that it be true. It is a rational premise, for example, that the existence of God would provide a purpose to the universe. He notes, as well, that not believing could mean missing out on the truth.

We know from modern science that intuitions are not infallible. Both James and Peirce had warned against certainty based on them. Neither James nor Peirce was a practicing Christian. James believed in the supernatural, but not in one God. Peirce's conception of God is somewhat vague. He doubted resurrection and immortality, but he believed in something more than the material world. Both, however, believed in the value of belief and Peirce said that far from being a vicious or a superstitious thing, it is simply a form of meditation.[18]

Pragmatists hypothesize, then, that God is not an actual or existent being but is nonetheless real in that belief in God gives purpose to the universe. Something is viewed as real, they suggested, by virtue of its consequences, that is, its usefulness. In "The Will to Believe," James defends belief despite the lack of evidence.

Though founded in instinct, God necessarily exists because non-existence is unintelligible is how the philosopher Charles Hartshorne (1897-2000) would explain it. The "general orderliness of the natural world is . . . difficult to reconcile with there being no Orderer." God is the Necessary Being.[19]

The above attempts to hypothesize God by way of intuition and reason are nothing new. Thinkers have always attempted to define God, as Robert Wright states in his book *The Evolution of God*. It is how religions are born. The very meaning of our lives depends on that definition.

According to Professor of Psychology Jordan Peterson, what we mean by "God" is the reality of the universe itself.[20] Societies define God in a way that makes sense as we try to function and give meaning to the world. In *Genesis*, God—Yahweh—is the spirit of order that goes out and conquers order. He is a hero, as is Marduk, slayer of the dragon of chaos in the Mesopotamian myth. When we encounter complete confusion, that is, chaos, the best thing to do is to apply language to create ideas or stories that conquer it.

---

[5] These terms, in order of appearance, are by John O'Donohue, Baruch Spinoza, Paul Tillich, C. S. Lewis, Moses Maimonides, and Saint Anselm.

[6] "Optimism and Pessimism," *The Essential Reinhold Niebuhr* (New Haven: Yale University Press,1986).

[7] Patrick Granfield, "An Interview with Reinhold Niebuhr," *commonwealmagazine.org* (December 16, 1966).

[8] "Marilynne Robinson in Conversation with Robert Hardies," YouTube (March 30, 2015).

[9] "Jordan B. Peterson and Sam Harris Debate God," YouTube.

[10] Andrew Ule, "Consciousness, Mind, and Spirit: Three Levels of Human Cognition," *core.ac.uk* (December 31, 2014), 494.

[11] William Desmond, "Introduction," Part Two, *The Examined Life*, ed. by Stanley Rosen (New York: Random House, 2000), 113.

[12] In his essay "Optimism and Pessimism."

[13] Lines from his poem "Auguries of Innocence."

[14] Massimo Pigliucci, "Rationally Thinking," *chem.tufts.edu* (Oct. 2002).

[15] David O'Hara, "The Sentiment that Invites Us to Pray," *irs. shanti.virginia.edu.*

[16] O'Hara.

[17] Jeff Jordan, "Pragmatic Arguments and Belief in God," *stanford.plato.edu* (Fall 2022 Edition), Edward N. Zalta & Uri Nodelman (editors).

[18] John R. Shook, "Peirce's Pragmatic Theology . . ." *pragmatism.org* (2011).

[19] "Charles Hartshorne," *plato.stanford.edu.*

[20] "Who Dares Say He Believes in God?" YouTube.

God as a Concept

Those believers who don't anthropomorphize God veer towards a "concept" rather than a "being," according to Karen Armstrong. In her book *The Case for God*, she traces the history of these concepts. For example, she writes that the seventeenth century philosopher Baruch Spinoza defined God as "an immanent force that wedded everything into unity and harmony." This is not a personal God, but the principle of Natural Law, "equivalent to the order that governs the universe."[21] According to Spinoza, God is a substance and that substance comprises everything in the universe. God needs to be thought of as an essence, not a corporeal being.[22]

The rabbis of Amsterdam expelled Spinoza for his views, considering him an atheist who replaced God with Nature, that is, a

Pantheist. His belief might more accurately be aligned with a doctrine called Panentheism. Panentheists "hold that God is present in and throughout nature and humans, but also transcends them and is much greater than them."[23] Panentheism is distinct from Pantheism in that it believes in a creator God. God is seen by the philosopher Charles Hartshorne, who called his belief Panentheism, as the Mind or Soul for the whole body of the natural world.

Panentheists believe that there is a Spirit in the world that is not only in nature but also transcends nature. The Spirit is not the Creator God of literal belief, but more akin to the "Brahman" of Hinduism's Vedanta school. Panentheistic conceptions of God can be found in most religions. Although Islam considers Pantheism a heresy, some Muslims in the mystical tradition have been considered panentheistic. The modern day theologian Mordecai Kaplan, whose work constitutes Reconstructionist Judaism, might also be

called a Panentheist. Panentheism strongly influenced the New England Transcendentalists,
like philosopher, essayist, and poet Ralph
Waldo Emerson, who wrote "The Oversoul."[24]
The ancient Greek philosopher Plato had
thought of the world as having such a Soul.

A Professor of Theology at Union
Theological Seminary, Roger Haight, a Jesuit
priest, conceives of God in a Panentheistic
way. His is not a Creator God, but a
Transcendent Presence. While present in the
world, God does not intervene. If God could
intervene, Panentheists ask, why would there
be evil in the world? God is not omnipotent,
in this panentheistic view. While not direct-
ing us step-by-step, this transcendent being
allows both free will and the evolutionary
process to work. It is the reason we are here. It
has shown that It cares for us by granting us
grace, leaving us free to accept it and become
awakened individuals. God works through
the teachings of individuals like Jesus Christ,

Moses, the Buddha, and Mohammad.[25] (This
is not Deism. Deists, who include some of
our founding fathers, most notably Thomas
Jefferson, believed that not only does God not
intervene, but also He is uncaring and distant.)

Arguably the greatest influence on modern
philosophers and liberal theologians was the
early twentieth century German philosopher
Martin Heidegger. Heidegger believed that
theism was dead, but he sought a path to a
new "God." We can seek this God in silence
and listening, in being present and in asking
questions: "What is imperatively needed,"
Heidegger thought, "is a radically new beginning which can induce silence and awe in us
before the mystery."[26] We humans participate
in history, he says, by questioning, by being
present and by discovering reality, the reality
that we call God. This approach is in opposi-
tion to metaphysical certitude; God is no longer the Designer. We can think of God as *Being*
working itself out. This concept incorporates a

role for evolution, which can be thought of as the universe becoming aware of itself.

Heidegger was looking for an anchor for the new historical world, that is, a world without the traditional God, certainly without traditional metaphors and certitude. For Heidegger, as for his contemporary, the renowned mathematician and metaphysician Alfred North Whitehead, "Creativity" is what produced it all; and, in keeping with evolutionary theory, the universe is moving towards more and more complexity. This is not to say that he argued for life after death, at least in an anthropomorphic sense. Arguments like Heidegger's present evolution as having a meaningful, though not supernatural, purpose, a meaning only to be discovered through silence.

While Heidegger can be viewed as an atheist, his philosophy inspired various Christians. In the twentieth century, after the discoveries of evolution and of Einstein, the Catholic scientist and theologian Pierre Teilhard de Chardin, a Jesuit priest, envisioned a modern story of creation. Teilhard saw the universe as a drama still being played out, still coming into being. It is awakening to "something indestructible," something that we can call God. God was not the beginning of the universe; rather, He is the goal of the universe. He is less the Alpha and more the Omega of the whole Cosmos. Teilhard pictured the universe as events in a story, not particles that disappear. He was a scientist (a paleontologist), as well as a mystic. He explained that his vision, which is more mystical than rational, was based on the sense of "rightness" that we all have.[27]

Other thinkers define God in similarly impersonal ways. Whitehead (1861-1947), for example, also thought of God as not separate from the world, but "in the world . . . continually creating in us and around us."[28] God might be thought of as a primordial essence.

Whitehead named God "Creativity" and is, moreover, credited with adding the term "creativity" to the dictionary.

Whitehead's ideas are known as "Process Theology" and have influenced everything from postmodern progressive theology to the ecological movement. He opposed religious dogma and criticized Christianity for turning God into a king or emperor; he would have preferred, he said, a God like the lowly Galilean—"persuasive and relational rather than controlling."[29]

For Whitehead, God is not omnipotent. God is a "fellow sufferer." We are held in His mind, but we are free to self-create. The world can enrich God just as God can enrich the world. Climate change, for example, is not in the hands of God. God can offer possibilities, but we humans have to fix it.[30] We can see in thinkers like Whitehead, who lived through the twentieth century's world wars, an attempt to reconcile God with the greatest evil. Interestingly, a similar attempt to discover a God that would make sense and work for believers had been the objective of William James, who had been one of Whitehead's mentors. James, too, had lived through a war, the American Civil War.

Not as a "being," but as "the Ground of Being" is how Paul Tillich, another influential Protestant theologian of the twentieth century, defines the concept of God. The "ground of being," the "power of being," the "unconditional," or our "ultimate concern" are his symbols for the Divine. God is not an object or a being, he argued. If a being, we would have to ask who created God. God is depth. God is our "ultimate concern." There is a very precious quality in things, which we call "God" and which we can access through "absolute commitment to ultimate truth, love, beauty, justice, and compassion."[31]

Tillich's God is a Presence, both transcendent and immanent. It is a "sustaining power." God is the energy that sustains the world. "God," as portrayed in the sacred texts, is a symbol of possibility—the possibility of the impossible. God is the mystery that promises a new and better life—renewal.[32]

Christ: For Christians, this unfolding of the universe in an ordered design is the will of God, made known to us through Jesus Christ. Christians believe that Jesus was divine, but also incarnate. In human form He represented what God wills for the world. Jesus is explained in the New Testament as the Word of God, or "*logos*." For believing Christians, it is Christ who comes out of Heidegger's void.

It was in the 1970s and 80s that liberal theologians, such as Karl Barth, first began to question the literal truth of Christ's portrayal in Scripture. They began to view miracles, including Christ's divinity, as metaphorical narratives. It was, in fact, primarily for his interpretation of Jesus that the Vatican took issue with Haight, a Jesuit priest. He sees Jesus as solely human, but one who experienced a more intense religious experience.[33] This view is not acceptable to traditional Christians.

Whether they believe that Christ was human or divine, it is His Divine message of compassion and forgiveness that draws both traditional and progressive Christians to their faith in God. The author and former editor of *The New Republic*, Andrew Sullivan, a progressive Catholic, believes in "Godness," a term he finds less anthropomorphic than "God." "Godness" is a "Force." It is moral truth, embedded in the universe and revealed to us through Jesus Christ. The choice is between Jesus and Nietzsche—between faith and nihilism.[34] His belief, which he calls an act of faith, comes to him admittedly in part from his Catholic upbringing. It is strengthened by mystical experience.

[21] New York: First Anchor Books, 2010, 200.

[22] Steven Nadler, "Baruch Spinoza," *stanford.plato.edu* (Summer 2022 Edition), Edward N. Zalta (editor).

[23] *www.pantheism.net/uuism.*

[24] "Panentheism," Wikipedia.

[25] "Grace-Filled Naturalism," an interview with Robert Wright, YouTube.

[26] Musa Duman, "Questioning and the Divine in Heidegger's *Beitrage*," 27: *Gatherings 2014* (GA 65: 262-63) on I-books.

[27] Prof. John Haught in an interview with Robert Wright, "The New Cosmic Story," YouTube.

[28] John Thatamanil, "Robert Wright and John Thatamanil," on YouTube (Apr. 2020).

[29] Thatamanil.

[30] Thatamanil.

[31] Armstrong, *The Case for God*, 283.

[32] John Caputo, "Theology of the Unconditional." YouTube.

[33] "Grace-Filled Naturalism."

[34] "Robert Wright and Andrew Sullivan," *The Wright Show*, YouTube.

Mysticism

In what ways other than through the teachings of prophets is God revealed to non-literal believers? While literal believers would cite miracles, non-literal believers might experience a reality they call God by way of mysticism.

Feeling God's presence cannot prove the existence of God, but for many it facilitates their leap to faith. For example, the argument from design grows out of "metaphysical astonishing at the aesthetic marvel of the happening of the world," a mystical experience. The experience has been described as "a deeper sensibility"—partly rational, partly feeling, a deep experience that something is holding reality there."[35]

The prophets of all religions, Jesus included, were "awakened" individuals. Their desire was to make the world a better place, society more attuned to those least fortunate, indeed, to all of suffering mankind. They attempted to do so by appealing to man's ability to transcend his own ego and perceive a more peaceful, harmonious world. This idealized vision is considered a mystical experience of God. Mystics, in effect, believe that we can transcend our egos and thereby experience a new reality. They believe in a Spirit that cannot be defined; one can only approach it intuitively. Their ideal vision can be called a World Soul.

Mystical experience is ecstasy. For Denys the Aeropogite, St. Paul's first Athenian convert, it was "intellectual rapture" that takes us where God is.[36] Meister Eckhart, the influential, medieval Christian mystic and theologian, wrote that the closer one gets to God, one's whole heart opens up. St. Augustine says something similar: "'. . . the light of steadfast trust poured into my heart, and all the shadows of hesitation fled away.'"[37]

William James asserted that all religious experience is mystical—ineffable. It involves a dissolution of the self so that one can connect to something beyond. Dissolving of the self is a common experience in Eastern religion. One might feel that the self/soul is identical with the eternal, absolute being. Eastern religions have always been less insistent on a personal God. One's life, it is believed, comes from "the ultimate energy that's the life of the universe."[38] Hindus call that source "Brahman." Other insights gained through mysticism might be called "union with God," "the oneness of all nature," "one's utter dependence on God," or the "impermanence of all things."

Some mediation is required for a mystical experience to occur, such as a religious tradition, a literature, or meditation. For

St. Anselm, the proof of God's existence is formulated in meditation—"a milieu of prayer."
Anselm was "a lover first and a theorist second."[39] Paul Tillich was moved to mystical
experience of God through art.[40] In Sufism, the
mystical tradition of Islam, it is the poetry of
Rumi that famously inspires mystical experience. In his love poetry, which for Persian-
reading mystics is second in importance
only to the Koran, one can find one's way to
Divinity.[41]

For the late twentieth century Irish poet
John O'Donohue, it is beauty that provides
mediation. Beauty ennobles the heart and the
heart apprehends God. "We feel most alive in
the presence of beauty." Humans are "hun-
gry for beauty." This sentiment is echoed by
Andrew Sullivan when he describes the light
and landscape of Cape Cod. He calls it the
immanence of God, or as mentioned above,
"Godness." It is what the Transcendentalists
Emerson and Henry David Thoreau felt.

Haight says that we have to go through "personal transformation" to grasp higher truths. One changes one's life as a result of mystical experience.[42] All contemplative schools, in fact, encourage transformation, a "quieting of the will," in order to move toward union with God.[43]

The Protestant theologian/philosopher Catherine Keller, a "process theologian" in the tradition of Whitehead, has said: "What is calling, what is luring—that is what we [process theologians] mean by 'God'."[44] Keller feels that the heart's deepest desire, what most lures us, is experience of a deep and abiding love. By entering into silence, one can find that love. It is God, but the experience goes beyond words. Human love has often been used analogously to describe the greater love that mystics apprehend in contemplation.

Whitehead was a mystic—he had a sense of a larger order of things. "What's wanted is an immense feeling for things, not a mind that requires facts."[45] Teilhard de Chardin also was a mystic. He believed in the human capacity to open ourselves to beyond what we can articulate. He envisioned the world as still coming into being, awakening to something indestructible, that is, to God.[46]

---

[35] Roger Haight, "Grace-Filled Naturalism." Robert Wright & Roger Haight, YouTube.

[36] Armstrong, *The Case for God*, 125-26.

[37] Armstrong.

[38] Campbell, "Masks of Eternity."

[39] William Desmond, "Introduction," *The Examined Life*, ed. by Stanley Rosen, 111.

[40] Nikkel, David, "The Mystical Formation of Paul Tillich," in *The Global Spiral* (December 5, 2006) *libris.uncg.edu.*

[41] "Sufism," *britannica.com.*

[42] "Grace-Filled Naturalism."

[43] David Bentley Hart, "Heaven, Hell, and Universal Salvation," Robert Wright and David Bentley Hart, YouTube.

[44] "Process and Prayer," YouTube.

[45] Amy Edelstein, "Alfred North Whitehead," YouTube.

[46] John Haught, ""The New Cosmic Story," Robert Wright & John Haught, YouTube.

Existentialist Mysticism

The insights into what mystics consider reality cannot be put into words. They propose that we can attribute nothing to a transcendent God through speech. God is totally beyond being, indescribable and ineffable. God is beyond all "things." He is "Nothing"—Nothing. He is an essence that permeates everything.[47] These are the sentiments of Paul Tillich. Tillich's theology grew out of the philosophy of Christian existentialists, particularly Søren Kierkegaard's.[48]

If God is Nothing, we are left in an abyss. This emptiness suggests meaninglessness, which causes great anxiety; but for Tillich, "vitality resists despair." He asserts that with "courage" we can get beyond this deep doubt. Through faith, one exemplifies a willingness to accept God. One accepts meaninglessness and thereby God appears, not the traditional God, but the God above God, the hidden God— Tillich's "Ground of Being." The final sentence in his famous book *The Courage to Be* asserts that faith is "rooted in the God who appears when God has disappeared in the anxiety of doubt." As the postmodern philosopher John Caputo puts it, Tillich's God "does not exist but insists."[49] In mystical experience we can find "an absolute assurance of the meaningfulness of one's life in the absence of any concrete evidence."[50]

For mystics, the abyss exudes meaning of all sorts. From this "cloud of unknowing," as it is called by Catherine Keller, "we find a 'luminous darkness' that brings a kind of epiphany of the mystery of God. This perspective serves to chasten our certitudes and dismantle our idolatries."[51] In the abyss, Keller finds Tillich's concept of Ground "unruly,"— made so, in part, by political and economic realities. She grapples with inequality and such dark concerns as racism, gender bias, and climate change. She envisions God as less fixed than Tillich's and more like Whitehead's. As a process theologian, she envisions God as "becoming." This viewpoint relieves the problem known as theodicy—the problem of evil. If God is "becoming"and the Cosmos is still unfolding—working things out—there is no omnipotent Being allowing evil to occur.

[47] Armstrong, *The Case for God*, 198-99.

[48] Aron Dunlop, "Are We Still Living in the Age of Anxiety?" YouTube.

[49] "Paul Tillich Symposium," YouTube.

[50] David H. Nikkel, "The Mystical Formation of Paul Tillich," *https://www.adwaitha-hermitage.net* (First published in *The Golden Spiral*, December 5, 2006).

[51] Anna Case-Winters, "Review" of Keller's *Cloud of the Impossible, journals.sagepub.com* (December 18, 2015).

The Moral Argument for the Existence of God

Another pathway to belief in God is the metaphysical argument from morality propounded by Immanuel Kant. He believed that our impulse to act morally, our sense of "unconditional good," leads to the necessary existence of a Perfect Being. If you watch people acting morally, Jordan Peterson explains, "there is divinity within us that reflects divinity itself."[52] As the Bible says, "We are made in the image of God."

We all intuit moral values. Different cultures might display some differences, but there is enough commonality to make assumptions about good and bad. We have deep, *a priori* intuitions.[53] This fact leads some to believe in God.

Marilynne Robinson is one who sees God in the moral behavior of humans, as well as in acts of kindness. Robinson has been deeply influenced by Jonathan Edwards, the American Puritan philosopher and preacher. She credits him for pursuing a "synthesis of the sacred and the beautiful," found in the beauty that human beings are capable of. The beautiful gesture of being generous, for example, brings a person closer to God. For Robinson this ethical standard is one of the most significant contributions of both John Calvin and Edwards. It was Edwards who said that "beauty is the signature of God in creation."[54] Moral behavior and beauty in all its forms are for some believers signs of divinity.

---

[52] "Jordan Peterson and Dennis Prager at the 2019 Prager U summit," YouTube.

[53] "Peterson vs. Sam Harris," Vancouver debate, YouTube.

[54] "Mind, Conscience, Soul," *What Are We Doing Here?* (New York: Farrar, Strauss and Giroux, 2018) 198.

Fathoming Faith

Religious faith is a feeling of confidence. The faithful believe it to be inspired by God—for Christians, it is a "gift" of God facilitated by "grace"; for Jews, a "spark" of Divinity bestowed on human beings; and for Muslims, "a knowledge in the heart." Theistic faith is the feeling of confidence that accompanies belief in a loving God.

Three components are fundamental to religious faith: (a) a psychological state, (b) a cognitive comprehension of the "truth," accepted without evidence, and (c) a practical commitment to one's religion.[55] Religious faith invokes the emotions, as well as reason, and a firm commitment. Believers find support for their faith by placing emphasis on one of the components, without neglecting the others. Different emphases among the faithful of how they understand their faith range from a transcendent experience of Divine reality, placing emphasis on the psychological experience, to a resolve to use "faith-commitment," with or even without belief, as simply a way to lead a good life.[56]

These understandings lead to what have been called "models" of faith.[57] The first model cares most for the effect of beliefs on one's psychological well-being. The acceptance of a benevolent transcendent reality induces calm, peace, even ecstasy for believers. The result is both physical and spiritual. [Faith] " … lives in and through the body but transcends it," wrote Reinhold Niebuhr.[58] Something "seizes one," says the philosopher John Caputo.[59]

The bliss arising from this state, however, is ordinarily grounded in some form of "knowledge," the cognitive element of faith, which accounts for the emphasis in a second model: "Faith as knowledge."[60] The "knowledge" that is relied upon might come from Holy Scripture and other sources of revelation, such as the prophets; but it might also derive from what philosophers and theologians have called "special knowledge."[61] Feeling God's presence and thus knowing that He exists can be characterized as a "quasi-perceptual" experience of God's presence. It is considered a gift from God and for the believer can result in certainty.[62]

Reformed epistemologists propose that this "higher cognitive faculty" was designed by God for the purpose of allowing believers to grasp theistic truth.[63] Calvin, for example, considered "knowledge" to be *recognition* of God made available through an innate religious sense.[64] When one believes, one interprets the world in a religious rather than a naturalistic sense. This ability to view the world religiously is a "special knowledge" account of faith that requires no further reasoning. It is something the believer experiences. The Protestant theologian Serene Jones, President of Union Theological Seminary, says that she experiences God's grace, which she understands as God's love. She feels that God is a living and loving presence in her life. This reality, she says, "grounds her and gives her the capacity to bear life." She believes, as Calvin did, that God is there if we choose Him, if we open our hearts to Him."[65]

One difficulty with justifying faith through this approach, however, is that it is evident only to the individual believer.[66] Is the revelation genuine? Moreover, there are possible natural explanations for such experience.[67]

Another means of "knowing" is by reasoning one's way to faith. Niebuhr would not assert that reason alone can prove the existence of God even though he sees a role for reason in man's search for meaning. "Faith allows us," he writes, "to make sense out of life by abstracting some eternal essence of man from the fragments of history."[68] The Christian faith assumes that humans are "capable of apprehending clues to the divine mystery and accepting the disclosure of the purpose of God."[69] Niebuhr would point to God's query addressed to Job in the Old Testament: "Who has endowed the earth with wisdom? Who has given understanding to the heart?"

While reasoning does not result in evidence of a scientific kind, philosophers have proposed that reason can provide assistance to belief in that knowledge gained by way of reasoning is not *contrary* to reason. The contemporary Catholic philosopher Professor Robert Audi, author of *Rationality and Religious Commitment*, reminds us that it could be rational to hold certain beliefs, even without evidence. On the problem of evil, for example, he has argued that God may not be "omnicompetent," especially in a world that is not considered deterministic. God would not have foreknowledge of the evil to be committed.[70]

Catholics, particularly, have appealed to the writings of Saint Thomas Aquinas, especially his "natural theology," which examines what we can say about God from a natural perspective, while excluding the supernatural, for example, proposing that a Designer is suggested by the order and beauty of the world. While it is understood, even by Aquinas, that this kind of reasoning is subject to error, it has lent support in the form of probability to many persons of faith. Aquinas, however, was of the opinion that faith is based on something between knowledge and opinion. One must first assent to the truth of the faith-claims. They might then be supported by reasoning. He concluded that "we come to know completely the truths of faith only through the virtue of wisdom (*sapientia*)," that "truth is of the Holy Spirit.'"[71]

For millennia, philosophers have appealed to a cosmological argument for the existence of a Creator. Aristotle proposed a First Cause, arguing that the universe could not have come from nothing. It is one of the five "proofs" for the existence of God put forth by Aquinas. Even the Big Bang theory, supported by modern science, could be interpreted as lending credence to the proposition of a Creator. Critics of the cosmological argument counter it with questions, such as, If a first cause is required, who created God? Or, If God is infinite, why then might it not be that energy always existed? If the argument is that something cannot come from nothing, a counter-argument is that energy existed and that the beginning of the universe had natural causes. As to the Big Bang, might it not have "shaped something" that was "already there?"[72]

Whereas the idea of a First Cause, a "Creator Being," has long been established in the West, in Eastern philosophy an alternative cosmological model has been adopted by Hindus, Buddhists, and Taoists. It proposes that there has never been "nothing." What exists is "energy that takes different forms" making the universe cyclical—eternally in flux. The "universe follows infinite, self-sustaining cycles."[73]

Other attempts to apply reason to the question of the existence of a Creator have been made through what is named a teleological argument— the "argument from design." The teleological argument proposes that given the order, complexity, and seeming purpose of nature, the universe had to have had a Designer. This intuition has led those who subscribe to it to use it as proof of the existence of a Deity.

Some of the arguments from design are as follows:

1.   The complexity of the universe implies purpose that suggests a supernatural Intelligence.

2.   "Scientists have determined that life in the universe would not be possible if more than about two dozen properties of the

universe were even slightly different from what they are."[74] That so much fine-tuning was necessary for the advent of biological life suggests a Designer as more probable than chance.

3.   The "religious experience" of those who believe and intuit a Designer can be taken as evidence. People of religious faith believe that this intuition has been "embedded in our thinking nearly naturally."[75]

Some of the counterarguments to a Designer hypothesis are as follows:

1.   The question arises: If a First Cause is necessary, who designed God? It can be asked *ad infinitum.*

2.   Physicists contend that "complex systems actually tend to be overly complex and would therefore be examples of poor design."[76] Then, too, if there is an

intelligent Designer, why is there so much waste in the universe? Why are there black holes and earthquakes?[77]

3. Arguments for ID (Intelligent Design) begin with the hypothesis that God exists.

4. Design could have been natural. Darwin's theory that biological design occurs naturally as living organisms evolve and adapt for survival has been accepted by most scientists.

5. The improbability of chance does not mean that the probability of an event is correct. The biologist Richard Dawkins, in fact, argues that the definition of improbability is "that which is difficult to explain." An Almighty God is more difficult to explain, he says, than is a natural chance event.[78]

6. Innate capacity to intuit design, that is, "religious experience," is not scientific evidence.

7.   The potential existence of multiverses is sometimes used as an argument in favor of chance, rather than a Designer, to account for the "fine-tuning" necessary for life in our universe. If there are innumerable universes, eventually one would become fine tuned enough for life. While the multiverses hypothesis is still highly speculative, some prominent physicists continue to test it.

Because none of the arguments that God exists is evidentially sound, possibly not even reasonable or probable since all of the arguments rely on predetermined belief, perhaps another model of faith is preferable for some.

Another approach to faith is to have faith "in God," not in the proposition that God exists.[79] Often, knowing and believing are not as significant to religious people as trust. This model of faith involves an "assent," a feeling of "rallying to [what one adopts as truth] with delight and engagement."[80] Central to it is "trust." The word "faith," as used in the New Testament, is, in fact, from the Greek *pistis*, which means "trust" or "commitment."[81] You have reasons to trust even when you don't understand, says Ross Douthat.[82] "Hoping against hope" is the way Saint Paul expressed this trust.

It would be considered rational (rational is not synonymous with "true") if that overriding trust can be seen as benefiting the person of faith. For example, one might trust in this way if one felt that salvation depended on it, a belief that might typically be instilled by growing up in a certain religion and being psychologically immersed in it.

Faith as trust might also be rational if it helps one to cope with life. Studies have shown that faith and the hope that accompanies it are healthful for us in various ways.

Serene Jones, for example, says that in a life full of suffering, even desolation, we create "the faith we need."[83] The Catholic feminist philosopher Mary Daly also turned to faith for comfort. It was from a state of loneliness or out of "aloneness and helplessness" that she came to believe in a personal God.

The Buddhist Sharon Salzberg wrote a book called *Faith: Trusting Your Own Deepest Experience,* in which she outlines how choosing faith over fear helps us to develop trust in ourselves and in life. For Andrew Sullivan, faith has become "a way of life." It is "how we treat people." He believes that tapping into the holiness that is built into the universe—what he calls "Godness"—helps one to be a better and happier person.[84] Similarly, Caputo calls his faith "a way to be."

William James, who was a renowned psychologist as well as a Pragmatist philosopher, saw faith as "the will to believe." James defended the "psychological possibility" of trusting that a proposition is true if that trust is beneficial. James later came to wish he had called his idea "the right to believe" because he did not think that one could will oneself to believe.[85] He thought that the natural state of man is to be happy and that sick souls could be cured by adopting faith. He viewed spiritual optimism as healthy minded and rational. James made positive thinking a cognitive therapy.

Others have commented on the healing power of faith in God. Carl Jung, for example, saw the Catholic faith as offering relief to sinners plagued by guilt.[86] St. Augustine had a restless soul until he surrendered to faith. "Our hearts are restless until they come to rest in Thee," he famously wrote. Through his faith, the great Russian novelist Leo Tolstoy discovered love for others. This compassion cured his own angst.

There is another form of faith that requires no belief in God, although belief is sometimes involved. John Dewey and James, for example, believed in some Ultimate Reality, but not in a personal God. Central to this faith option is a commitment to "a line of conduct." It defines faith as "treating hoped for and unseen things as if they were real and then acting accordingly."[87] "Behave as if metaphysical truth...were true and you will come out ahead," says Jordan Peterson.[88] It could turn out to be a particularly important way of having religious faith in the future.[89]

Finally, there are those who are uncertain about the theist proposition, but want it to be true. Their commitment is to hope. It can even be seen as a "virtue of personality."[90] What is hoped for is salvation, as well as the triumph of Goodness or Love. Again, it necessarily involves firm commitment.

It is worth noting that while their forms of commitment vary, eighty-one percent of Americans say they believe in God. It can be noted, however, that this number of believers is at a new low.[91]

---

[55] "Faith," *plato.stanford.edu*. Section 1.

[56] "Faith," Sections 2 & 8.

[57] "Faith," Section 1.

[58] *Major Works*, 6.

[59] "Theory of the Unconditional," YouTube.

[60] "Faith," Section 3.

[61] "Faith," Section 4.

[62] "Faith," Section 3.

[63] Plantinga, Alvin, *Warranted Christian Belief* (New York: Oxford University Press, 2000). Cited in "Faith."

[64] Paul Helm, "On Calvin," part 3: *Knowledge of God and of Ourselves, theguardian.com* (12 October 2009).

[65] "Call It Grace," Robert Wright & Serene Jones, YouTube.

[66] "Faith," Section 4.

[67] "Faith," Section 5.

[68] "Foolishness of the Cross," *Major Works*, 827.

[69] "Mystery and Meaning," *Major Works*, 768.

[70] "The Problem of Evil," YouTube.

[71] "St. Thomas Aquinas," *iep.utm.edu*.

[72] Victor J. Stegner, quoted in Philip A. Pecorino, *Introduction to Philosophy*, Chapter 3. *qcc.cuny.edu*.

[73] Stegner.

[74] "Design Arguments for the Existence of God," *iep.utm.edu.*

[75] "Teleological Arguments for God's Existence," s*tanford. plato.edu.*

[76] Mark Perakh, quoted by Mark D. Decker, "Why Intelligent Design Isn't Intelligent," <u>Cell Biology Education</u>, Vol. 4, 121-122, Summer 2005.

[77] Alfred Pecorino, *Introduction to Philosophy,* Chapter 3, *qcc. cuny.edu.*

[78] Pecorino.

[79] "Faith," Section 6.

[80] "Faith," W. C. Smith is quoted.

[81] Armstrong, *The Case for God*, 87.

[82] "Andrew Sullivan and Ross Douthat debate Bad Religion," YouTube.

[83] "Call It Grace."

[84] "Robert Wright and Andrew Sullivan."

[85] "Faith," Section 7.

[86] Jordan Peterson, "The Death and Resurrection of Jesus Christ," YouTube.

[87] F. R. Tennant quoted in "Faith," Section 8.

[88] Peterson, "Peterson and Harris debate," YouTube.

[89] J.L. Schilling quoted in "Faith," Section 8.

[90] "Faith," Section 10.

[91] "How Many Americans Believe in God?" *news.gallup.com* (June24, 2022).

Hope

A commitment to the Divine is usually accompanied by theological hope. Faith and hope go hand-in-hand. The Christian existentialist Søren Kierkegaard recognized that faith in God leads to hope for eternity.[92] Human beings in any case are hopeful by nature, most probably in order to ward off fear; and we base our hope not on certainty, but on probability. No particular hope is irrational, however, according to Kant, "as long as its object cannot be proven to be impossible."[93] We cannot hope for something we believe is impossible.

For the American author and *New York Times* columnist Ross Douthat, Heaven is real. While acknowledging intellectual difficulties and doubt, this politically neoconservative Catholic also appreciates the transcendence his faith provides; and he remains hopeful that one day we will be "transfigured." "There's going to be a new Heaven and a new Earth," he said recently. Moreover, he asserts, "if He [God] made us at all," we will be as we are—not spirits. He points out that "Christianity is extraordinarily hopeful."[94] One of the officiates at Senator John McCain's funeral echoed this hope when he ended his eulogy with the Christian prayer: "Let eternal life be our hope."

Even though he doesn't believe in a literal heaven, the religious poet Christian Wiman says that Heaven "keeps asserting itself in my imagination." For him it is a way of surviving. But it is not so much hope in a specific place, but rather a general feeling. Wiman cites the Irish poet Seamus Heaney as saying that hope is a condition of your soul.[95] Many think of it as an attitude. Mystics transcend a condition of emptiness into a more meaningful and hopeful condition. Hope is a kind of energy. It becomes a habit that keeps us going.

"Whether we like it or not, hope is written so deeply into our hearts that we just can't help ourselves, no matter how hard we try otherwise," says Supeap, a character in Camron Wright's novel *The Rent Collector*. When Marilynne Robinson's character Reverend Ames baptizes his young wife, he calls the condition of Hope "sweet," using the Christian baptismal phrase "the sweetness of hope."[96]

According to Saint Paul, it was Abraham who, amidst the tremendous suffering of his people, exemplified "hope against hope." This hope has become the core of the Judeo-Christian tradition.

Jews speak less of an afterlife than traditional Christians do, taking the view that "Someday we'll know." Hope, however, remains powerful in their worldview. They concentrate their faith and hope on making this a better world. "*Tikuun olam*" is the task of "restoring the world"—"healing the world one heart at a time."[97]

In spite of the significance of hope in a religious sense, an ambivalent attitude towards hope as a virtue is at least as old as the ancient philosophers. While Plato warned against a "gullible" hope, he conceded that some pleasure can be taken from hope, or "anticipation," as he worded it, if there is a chance that our hope will be realized. Aristotle likewise viewed hope with varying degrees of enthusiasm. Having hope, he felt, doesn't necessarily lead one to have courage, a virtue he strongly extolled. It might, in fact, provoke anxiety in some who are "at sea [. . .] and in disease." However, when hope creates confidence, which he believed "is the mark of a hopeful disposition," it then sustains courage.[98]

Seneca and the Stoics had no use for hope, the opposite of which they considered fear. Since both hope and fear are passions, they believed, they should be overcome. "According to Seneca, we should avoid both fear and hope and instead focus on the present and cultivate tranquility of the soul."[99]

In the famous Greek myth, Pandora opens her box and allows every ill that mankind suffers to be unleashed on the world except one. That she held back the goddess Hope has been interpreted in various ways over the centuries. Was Hope preserved in order to help mankind or did the Greeks consider her to be misleading. The renowned classicist Robert Graves agrees with the latter interpretation. He regards the goddess Hope, who was left in Pandora's jar, as "delusive."

Buddhists have the same ambivalence. Like some of the ancient philosophers, however, Buddhists distinguish between hope that is simply a desire for something specific and the emotion that could be called "wise hope." An enlightened person would be free of hope that can be defined as craving. That kind of hope is a form of suffering. "Wise hope" is a radical and unconditional aspiration to rise above suffering by facing reality and addressing it.[100]

The psychiatrist and theologian Gerald May has termed this "wise," transcendent religious hope as "naked hope" or "contemplative hope." It is not simply craving or desire, emotions that can lead to disappointment. May found "wise" hope in people he met in Bosnia who had lost everything and still retained a deep hope:

"Yes, hope," they smiled.

I asked if it was hope for peace.

"No, things have gone too far for that."

I asked if the United Nations or the United States would intervene in some positive way.

"No, it is too late for that."

I asked them, "Then, what is it you are hoping for?"

They were silent. They could not think of a thing to hope for. Yet, there it was—undeniable hope shining in them.

I asked one last question: "How can you hope when there is nothing to hope for?"

The answer was, *"Bog"*—the Serbo-Croatian word for God.[101]

"All hope is as fragile as glass," wrote Vitoria Colonna, the poet and friend of Michelangelo.[102] Yet humans cling to it. The young neurosurgeon, Paul Kalinithi, writes in his memoir that "hope" denotes "some combination of confidence and desire." His hope was for a cure. Even while he was dying of terminal cancer, he still remained hopeful.[103]

While the Stoics might consider hope to be a weakness equivalent to fear and while the author Albert Camus considered hope "absurd" in an "absurd world," particularly eternal hope, most psychologists agree that a hopeful attitude is motivational and good for us as long as it is reasonable, as long as it is guarded, and as long as it doesn't become an out of control emotion or passion. It remains, in any case, significantly attached to religious faith in that believers hope for a Divine significance to the world. Such hope may be ardent, but must, by its nature, walk hand-in-hand with doubt.

[92] "Hope," *plato.stanford.edu.* Section 2.5.

[93] "Hope."

[94] "Andrew Sullivan & Ross Douthat."

[95] "How Does One Remember God?" *onbeing.org* (January 4, 2018).

[96] In the novel *Lila.*

[97] Rachel Naomi Remen, "How We Live with Loss," *onbeing.org.*

[98] "Hope,"*plato.stanford.edu.*

[99] "Hope."

[100] Roshi Joan Halifax, "Yes, We Can Have Hope," *lionsroar.com* (May, 2020).

[101] Marcia Ford, *Cultivating God's Gift of a Hopeful Spirit*, xi-xii.

[102] Translated by Abigail Brundin.

[103] *When Breath Becomes Air* (US: Random House, 2016) 133.

Pantheism

Pantheism is a doctrine that denies a personal God, but proposes that God is Nature itself. Pantheists accept an intuition that God and the world are one and the same, that they overlap. For Pantheists, the Cosmos is self-created and goes on nurturing the world, including humans.

To Pantheists the universe is a living, conscious, purposeful entity. It is natural, not supernatural, materialistic, but also spiritual. Pantheists think of God as the immanent vitality of the world.

Pantheists do not generally use anthropomorphic descriptions of God. Some traditional Pantheists, however, have given Nature a mind-like capacity. The 17th century philosopher Baruch Spinoza, the most famous figure in traditional Pantheism, felt that there exists a "substance" that could extend beyond what we can grasp. It created the world and sustains the world. Thus, neither he nor Einstein, who believed in Spinoza's God, called themselves atheists. Spinoza felt that God is an all-knowing "infinite intellect." Being deterministic, Spinoza's view denies free will. His God also has no purpose in mind. While necessarily nurturing "Its" own creation, It could never love the world. The way we know this God is intuitive. Spinoza proposed that intuitive insight "enables us to grasp the essence of things."[104]

Those with a pantheistic view of the world perceive a unity pervading the Cosmos, which includes human beings. These feelings give rise to a sense of holiness and moral order. The Cosmos is to be deeply revered. It is the divine quality of the universe, the marvelousness of it, that moves Pantheists to revere nature. Its ultimate mystery inspires awe. One feels love for it and gratitude. If a Pantheist construes the universe as aware or as extending to a non-physical consciousness, [105] it makes sense that one could even pray to and petition it. Considering that human beings are a part of the world, one could be said to be petitioning the God within oneself.

Famous writers who have espoused pantheistic views include Goethe, Wordsworth, Emerson, and Walt Whitman. Popular culture also explores pantheistic themes in movies such as *Star Wars*. The religious traditions of Hinduism's Advaita Vidanta school, Kabbalistic Judaism, Celtic spirituality, and Sufi mysticism have strong "pantheistic ideas and feelings." [106]

Pantheism is not paganism, which endorses belief in gods and goddesses; nor is it pansychism, the view that all matter has consciousness; and it is not even panentheism, a theistic doctrine that allows for free will and represents God as including the world, not as being the world.

The contemporary philosopher Robert Corrington has written of a "deep pantheism" that he calls "Ecstatic Naturalism." He defines God or Nature as the spirit or energy that makes "worldhood" possible.[107] The universe he proposes is divine, albeit not omnipotent. We experience the immanence of divinity (sacredness) in the universe through epiphanies—"epiphanies of the holy"—or as "the lure for personal and communal transformation." He uses terms like "God" and the "Divine," but he is referring to Nature, not the supernatural. Nature is all there is. It has no purpose, only what Arthur Schopenhauer termed a "will to life."[108] Like Emersonian, post-Christian nature spirituality, his thought is inspired by Hinduism. Some sects of Hinduism can be interpreted as pantheistic.

God / Nature / the Universe is the energy that allows individuality to "flower," by way of *"agape,"* or Divine love. Corrington says that this process is called "selving." ("Selving" is a concept formulated by the late 19th century, Catholic poet Gerard Manley Hopkins that signifies a drive within each order of nature to fulfill itself.) Absolute spirit lies beneath all orders of the world, including the divine." God (Nature) is neither a supernatural being nor omnipotent, but "It" sustains the world.

Traditional Pantheists think of the world as God. Another contemporary form of Pantheism is naturalistic or scientific, a cosmic pantheistic view that leaves out belief in God. Scientific Pantheists believe that the universe is divine in that it is awe inspiring, without reference to any Creator beyond nature. It rejects any anthropomorphism, such as the possibility that nature could love humans as a father loves his offspring. Divinity is not conceived of as a person. Scientific Pantheism also disallows immortality, but its believers "do not feel horror of the prospect of dissolution back into nature at the time of their individual deaths."[109]

Pantheism is known to be extremely compatible with the values of Unitarian Universalism, a liberal religion where some believe in God and some do not. They promote values, not metaphysical hypotheses. People of faith or no faith find a home in this tradition. "Members often add their own beliefs from various religions. Up to a third or half are sympathetic to Pantheism.[110]

[104] "Pantheism," *plato.stanford.edu.*

[105] Wang-Eun Serling, *A Consciousness Study Comparing Robert Corrington, Yu Young-Mo, and Henry Stapp, digitalcollections. drew.edu.* 2019.

[106] "Pantheism."

[107] *Nature and Spirit: An Essay in Ecstatic Naturalism* (New York: Fordham University Press, 1992) 32-33.

[108] "Robert Corrington," *Wikipedia.*

[109] Garrett, Jan, "An Introduction to Pantheism," *peoplewku.edu.*

[110] "Pantheism and Unitarian Universalism," *ww.pantheism. net/uuism.*

Buddhism

Another prevalent spiritual worldview, as well as a religion for some, is Buddhism. Orthodox Buddhists believe in rebirth, as well as in *karma*; and they frequent temples to pray to gods. Many Buddhists worldwide, even in the United States, according to polls conducted by *pewforum.org*, believe in a Universal Spirit. Many modern day Buddhists, however, view Buddhism as a secular religion. They approach it as a lifestyle, psychologically therapeutic by virtue of its worldview and its discipline of mindfulness. While some secular Buddhists are actively anti-theistic, others adopt an agnostic view.

Whether traditional or secular, Buddhists place paramount importance on the Buddha's teachings, known as the *Dharma*. The Buddha died in the fourth century BCE, and there was no written form of his teachings until the Pali Canon, written in the Pali language during the first century BCE. Although he had been raised in an aristocratic Hindu family that probably held ancient Indian religious beliefs, the Buddha ultimately decided that the gods were not helpful in his quest to determine how people could alleviate their suffering. What we know of the Buddha and his beliefs, of course, is dependent on the accuracy of oral transmission. The so-called Early Buddhist Texts, however, were memorized by monks highly skilled at memorization and were passed down in the form of chants or *sutras*.

After many years of contemplation, the Buddha himself reached a point of enlightenment when he discovered four principles of existence known as the Four Noble Truths. They are the essence of Buddhism, and they are as follows:

1. Existence is suffering. (Suffering is often defined as "dissatisfaction" or "unsatisfactoriness.")

2.   Suffering has a cause, namely craving, desire, and attachment. Craving pleasure, material goods, and immortality can only continue what is an ultimately unquench-able thirst. Eventually, craving itself be-comes an unhealthy mental state.

3.   A cessation of suffering can be achieved by "letting go." Pleasures are real, but must be recognized as fleeting in order to reduce one's craving for them.

4.   There is a path to the cessation of suf-fering, an enlightened path known as "The Eightfold Path" that helps one to "let go" of craving. It consists of eight practices: right views, right resolve, right speech, right action, right livelihood, right effort, right mindfulness, right concentration.

The tradition that is the most widely prac-ticed form of Buddhism in the United States is the Theravada Vipassana tradition imported from Burma. It is otherwise known as Insight Meditation. Along with other schools or traditions of Buddhism, like Zen Buddhism, for example, it relies, with some variation of interpretation, on Buddhism's metaphysical view of existence. Most significantly, Buddhists believe there are three marks to existence—impermanence, suffering or "unsatisfactoriness," and "not-self."

Each of these marks of existence has been the subject of much philosophical discussion and deserves at least some explication.

<u>Impermanence</u>: All things are impermanent. Life changes and is changeable. When you observe things objectively and see the flowing nature of life, your life becomes manageable.

<u>Suffering</u>: All existence is suffering, in large part due to its impermanence, but also to restless longing for something in the future

that we think will bring happiness, but the attainment of which usually results in even more longing. Staying on "the path," that is, the path to enlightenment, will bring relief. As Robert Wright (*Why Buddhism Is True*) points out, the Buddha discovered this reality, which today is known as the "hedonic treadmill," long before modern day cognitive psychologists.[111]

Not-self: All existence is "not-self." The self that we identify with is not what we think it is. Above all, it is not fixed and permanent.

Although one knows that the persona that one presents to the world is not one's true self, one usually believes in an inner self, one's real identity. This, too, is "not-self." The Buddha teaches that the self is an assemblage of five aggregates: the body, feelings, thoughts, perceptions, and consciousness. These entities interact with each other; for example, our feelings influence our thoughts. The result is a momentary conglomerate, but it is fluid. The "self" is not a fixed entity, but rather a process. The aggregates come together moment by moment in an ongoing construction that the monk/scholar Bhikku Bodhi calls "selfing."[112]

One of the aggregates is consciousness, which is "special because it has the capacity for subjective experience." Awareness "gives life meaning" and gives "valence to moral questions."[113] However, it is just one part of the "self" that comes together momentarily in the ongoing flux of "selfing." Mindfulness meditation teaches the Buddhist not to cling to the view of a fixed self and to view who we think we are with an open mind and a sense of non-attachment.

The self is also not in control. The Buddha would have us stop thinking of ourselves as having what Wright calls a "CEO" who is "calling the shots." Buddhism teaches that we need to let go of this "tightly constructed self" and let it flow, by way of open and direct experience. This way we find that we are interconnected and interdependent. Liberating oneself of one's ego allows one to grasp that other people are as important as oneself. It's not all about "me." This letting go relieves anxiety and fosters a connection that leads to compassion, not only for others, but for oneself. Wisdom arrives, according to the Buddha, the moment you do away with the self and recognize your connectivity.

---

[111] Robert Wright, *Why Buddhism Is True* (US: Simon & Schuster, 2017) 10.

[112] "Immanent Buddhism," Robert Wright and Bhikku Bodhi, *Meaning of Life*, YouTube.

[113] *Why Buddhism Is True*, 90.

Secular Buddhism

Some modern Buddhist teachers have whittled down the doctrines of Buddhism to what they consider to have been most relevant to the Buddha, as well as to what is most helpful to twentieth-century practitioners. The former Buddhist monk Stephen Batchelor is one such secular teacher (*Buddhism without Beliefs*). On theological questions, such as rebirth, he is an agnostic. In his books, he instead turns to the earliest Buddhist texts to discover what the Buddha taught and how it relates to modern Buddhists.

The Buddha was not interested, Batchelor writes, in offering us consolation by way of dogmatic religious belief, but rather through engagement with mystery, perplexity, and doubt. The core of the *Dharma* is ethical. The Buddha, he contends, had envisioned a task-based ethical practice. The religion shifted into a metaphysics after the Buddha's death.[114]

To summarize his findings Batchelor invented the apt acronym ELSA. Wright calls the content "Buddhism in a nutshell." The acronym stands for Embrace/Let go/Stop/Act. *Embrace* life in all its dimensions, including suffering. *Let go* of instinctive reactions such as fear (aversion to bad feelings) and greed (clinging to good feelings). *Stop* reacting and come to rest in a clear, non-reactive state of mind. <u>Act</u>: embark on an ethical life (by way of the Eightfold Path).

Batchelor believes that Buddhism works, especially in its practice of mindfulness meditation. Mindfulness is the practice of paying attention to the phenomenal world, including one's own mental states and feelings, not transcendence to some out-of-sight reality.[115] Meeting every person and every experience with deep surprise and puzzlement allows one to let go of pre-conceived notions.[116] The scholar Erik Braun describes mindfulness in a similar way—paying attention with non-elaborative, non-judgmental acceptance of the moment.[117]

According to Batchelor, the "sutras," which are among the earliest Buddhist texts, suggest that mindfulness will get us to engage in the world in a selfless way—open, empathetic, present, and non-reactive.

Batchelor believes that Buddhism speaks to the needs of the people at any given time. When it goes into various countries, it reinvents itself. Batchelor's emphasis is on mindfulness meditation because it helps one to achieve serenity. The way the modern world pressures us to produce and achieve is "almost violent at times," he says.[118] Although mindfulness is only one step in the Buddha's path to enlightenment, one needs to be mindful while working on the other steps. Mindfulness is basic to following the Eightfold Path.

Mindfulness is one kind of meditation, according to Joseph Goldstein, a longtime meditator and a cofounder of the Insight Meditation Center in Barre, Massachusetts. It is not aiming for the spiritual ecstasy that can accompany deep concentration, Goldstein says, but rather for clarity of thinking, or wisdom. It helps us to accept the impermanence of all things, as well as to decondition ourselves from habitual patterns that create our suffering.

Goldstein also stresses the strong ethical nature of Buddhist insight. He says that mindfulness is always a "wholesome" state.[119]

When the Buddha realized that there is a path to the cessation of suffering, he is said to have been enlightened. Goldstein defines enlightenment as liberation from greed, fear, and delusion. He expands on greed as "addictive wanting," as craving/attraction/clinging. Fear includes aversion to suffering, but also hatred, ill will, irritation, and other reactive feelings, which would not arise if one were enlightened. Delusion is ignorance of the reality of existence.

After one commits to the process of awakening through the Buddha's practical regimen, one can achieve enlightenment. One who is enlightened has become aware of the impermanence, craving, and "not-self" that make up existence. One becomes enlightened before entering the state of *nirvana*, which is the cessation of suffering.

For a traditional Buddhist, *nirvana* would be entering into the flow of the universe. One would no longer be subject to rebirth and its consequent suffering. Reinhold Niebuhr defined it as mystical, as transforming the self until it has achieved "the universality of the divine."[120] Karen Armstrong suggests that it is analogous to God.[121]

Secular Buddhists either redefine *nirvana* as "equanimity"or dismiss it as a metaphysical part of traditional Buddhism. According to Bhikku Bodhi, however, a transcendent realization is at least possible for secular Buddhists if they accept the principles even while denying the supernatural concepts of rebirth; *karma*, the sum of one's actions, which determines one's level of rebirth; and transcendent *nirvana*. Few reach the total cessation of suffering, but there is a spectrum of awakening to enlightenment as one rids oneself of negative actions and the negative emotions that lead to them. Even the wisest of human beings need time to see clearly. Think of Abraham Lincoln and his evolving views on slavery.[122]

---

[114] "Wondrous Doubt," *onbeing.org.*

[115] "Secular Buddhism," Robert Wright and Stephen Batchelor, Meaning of Life, YouTube.

[116] "Wondrous Doubt."

[117] "The Birth of Insight," Robert Wright & Erik Braun, YouTube.

[118] "Wondrous Doubt."

[119] In his book *Mindfulness* and on YouTube videos.

[120] *Essential Niebuhr*, 221.

[121] *The Case for God*, 33.

[122] "Immanent Buddhism."

Spirituality

Human experience tells us there is more to reality than materialism. One is not fully human without a spiritual dimension. Jon Kabat-Zinn has defined spirituality as "what it means to be deeply human."[123] A "spiritual dimension is necessary to human beings," the interviewer and author Krista Tippett once said when discussing the beautiful poetry of John O'Donohue.[124] In an interview published in *The Guardian*, Sam Harris, author, neuroscientist, and militant atheist, said: "We need to live our lives with more than just facts."[125]

Many people today consider themselves spiritual but not religious. We know what they mean when they say they are "not religious," that is, not strictly adhering to the doctrines of a specific religion. The term "spiritual," however, is more ambiguous. At one time spirituality was attached to religious experience and the soul. To be spiritual was akin to being mystical. For some time now the definition of the term has been expanding into secular life. Some spiritual teachers, in fact, do not like the term because of its application to such a wide array of experiences.[126] Most thinkers on the subject, however, agree that one can be spiritual without being religious.

Firstly, the term "spiritual" derives from a Greek word that means "air," "breath," or "spirit." Religious spiritualists who believe in the supernatural refer to the spirit as the soul, an eternal being that connects one to the Divine. Secular spiritualists adhere to the human spirit, that which connects one to her/his higher self. The "higher self" is "the impersonal [non-egoistic], universal or higher component of human nature."[127]

The spiritual person, with or without recourse to the supernatural, engages the part of herself or himself that seeks to find meaning in life. The goal of life for all of us is to be happy, and a spiritual person finds happiness in spiritual ways. Most psychologists agree that a spiritual way of life is more gratifying than a purely materialistic way of life. Being spiritual is a way to experience satisfaction, even bliss. Additionally, a person's being spiritual can benefit others because a spiritual person has a conscience.

A secular spiritual person's focus is on values like "love, compassion, caring, fellowship, tolerance, respect for and willingness to understand and coexist with other traditions and religions, responsibility, apathy for material abundance, and social harmony without commitment to a personal God or an impersonal Absolute."[128] Spirituality is activation not of belief but of the human spirit.

There is a spectrum on which individuals might measure themselves as somewhere between non-spiritual and wholly spiritual. Few of us achieve enlightenment or sainthood; some of us, in fact, not having had any experience with spiritual transcendence, might consider ourselves low on the spirituality spectrum.

---

[123] "'Secular' mindfulness as deeply Buddhist," Robert Wright & Jon Kabat-Zinn, YouTube.

[124] "John O'Donohue: The Inner Landscape of Beauty," *onbeing.org.*

[125] "Sam Harris, the new atheist with a spiritual side," *theguardian.com* (February 16, 2019).

[126] "Secular Mindfulness as deeply Buddhist," Robert Wright & Jon Kabat-Zinn. Zinn is Professor of Medicine *emeritus* and creator of the Center for Mindfulness at the University of Massachusetts.

[127] "Human spirit," Wikipedia.

[128] *Morality and Spirituality in the Contemporary World,* ed. by Chandana Chakrabarti and Sandra Jane Fairbanks, "Preface," *vii-viii. cambridgescholars.com.*

Love, Wonder, and Self-Transcendence

Notably, thinkers who define authentic spirituality agree on three essential qualities that a spiritual person exhibits. One is compassion, often defined as "boundless love." Another is awe or wonder, leading to humility and gratitude. Finally, spirituality requires self-transcendence, leading to connectedness. These qualities overlap; that is, where you find one you will most often find the others.

Love is the foremost spiritual emotion. It leads to other spiritual values. Author-scholar Karen Armstrong notes its importance to all religions: "All faiths insist that compassion is the first step of true spirituality and that it brings us into relation with the transcendence we call God, Brahman, Nirvana, or Dao."[129]

Armstrong inspires compassion in others and helps us define it as a spiritual value. In 2008, after winning the TED prize, she called on people around the world to help her launch a Charter for Compassion. It is currently available in thirty languages and millions of people have endorsed it. Its supporting organization is called Charter for Compassion International, which partners with hundreds of organizations in sectors from the arts to science, from business to peace and justice.[130]

Armstrong believes that "spirituality" refers to the qualities that inspire us to do what is right and good—for ourselves and others. Included in the Charter is a list of what she calls "spiritual assets." Some of them are the following:

- Being charitable toward others
- Being compassionate
- Appreciation and gratitude
- Spreading hope

- Sharing hospitality
- Practicing humility
- Advocating for justice
- Patience: enduring trials
- Showing tolerance and acceptance

One of the supporting partners in the Charter for Compassion organization is the Spiritual Paths Foundation, which provides inter-spirituality courses and lectures largely devoted to the contemplative life. It was founded by Ed Bastian, a prolific author, professor, and lecturer, and practitioner of Buddhist meditation. Bastian says that spiritual people struggle to fulfill the deepest human yearning, that is, "to know who we are, to be in tune with the deepest principles, and ethics, and wisdom brought to us from our elders and that we intuitively grasp."[131] Early in his life Bastian felt inspired by the wisdom of the Dalai Lama, who has said: "If you want others to be happy, practice compassion. If you want to be happy, practice compassion."

In addition to love, the spiritual person experiences awe and wonder at life. It is exhibited as humility when contemplating the universe, as well as appreciation of our existence. Contemplating the mystery of existence in this way is a spiritual experience.

Two of America's foremost physicists are inspired by wonder to learn more about the Cosmos. For Brian Greene, professor of physics and mathematics at Columbia University, spirituality is having a deep emotional response to contemplation of the Cosmos.[132] It is awe at the ability of mathematics and physics to advance our knowledge of the Cosmos that leads him to continue searching for the truth of existence.

Responding to the immense beauty of the Cosmos—its symmetry and design, another scientist, Nobel-Prize-winning physicist Frank Wilczek, says, "The world is a work of art." There is truth in the beauty of the universe.

Evolution has primed us to enjoy it. Through science we begin to sense who we are. We can enrich our lives by sensing our place in the world. The mystery can be humbling.[133]

Most of us feel moved by the wonder and beauty of nature. Nature has long inspired spiritual experience. Becoming caught up, even blissful, in nature is a common experience. It is a spiritual experience in that it connects us to the natural world, thereby increasing our appreciation for it. We care about it as we care about ourselves. We know that as part of nature, we need to respect it and live in harmony with it.

Spiritual experiences nourish the human spirit—the heart and mind. Aesthetic experiences are spiritual experiences. Music and art transport us by their beauty, and strike us as reflections of reality. Mathematicians, too, find gateways to spirituality, for example, in the study of patterns.[134]

When we have such experiences as compassion for others, humility at the mystery of existence, and gratitude for life, we are experiencing self-transcendence, the third essential quality of spiritual experience. To embrace authentic spirituality one must be capable of transcendence—transcendence of materialistic craving and of ego. Transcendence is, in fact, a state we all enjoy at times. It is ecstasy, stepping outside of our mundane world, finding value in life.[135]

Self-transcendence means rising above self-interest and recognizing humanity's interdependence. An experience of oneness is in all spiritual traditions. It does not exclude the self as part of that universe, but it insists on a perspective that includes others. That it's not "all about me," is how Robert Wright has explained the Buddhist concept of "not-self."

Sam Harris writes: "It is quite possible . . . to experience a kind of boundless, open awareness —to feel—in other words, at one with the cosmos." In an enchanting analogy, Harris suggests that one think of oneself as transparent, like a "bubble in the sea." We take care of ourselves and our loved ones, but we can apprehend that we are still part of the sea.[136]

In *Man's Search for Meaning*, Victor Frankl, the Austrian psychiatrist who spent time in concentration camps during WWII, likewise speaks of spirituality as transcendent and of the spiritual person as an "aware" being who "reveals, connects, unites and comprehends the existence of another being."[137]

Although Western religions have their mystical tradition, Eastern religions long preceded us in appreciation of the human capacity for experiencing transcendence and feeling as one with the universe. It was Hinduism that first inspired non-Christian spirituality in the West. For Hindus, the Ultimate Reality is Brahman, while the part of humans known as Atman, an eternal self, is only temporarily separated from Brahman. The goal is for them to be re-united in the Oneness that is the nature of the universe.

It is also from the East that we have been taught to meditate in order to achieve a higher consciousness. Mindfulness meditation may for some simply be stress reducing; however, for others, like Harris, who is a neuroscientist, it is the portal to enlightened awareness. Meditating affords him a clearer picture of reality and a better understanding of consciousness. Indeed, for Harris, who spent twenty years in silent retreats in India, spirituality is inseparable from consciousness. Even though consciousness is a mystery, he has said, in that we don't understand "why the lights suddenly came on," we know we have it and it is through it that we transcend the self. By training our minds, we become "more focused, patient, and compassionate than one naturally tends to be."[138]

"Ascent of the spirit"—through physical centers of experience called chakras—is, in fact, basic to Buddhism and Hinduism.[139] The practice anticipates the mind-body connection of contemporary science. Early texts in both of these Eastern religions describe the ritual of opening a person's seven chakras, which are located in various parts of the body, in order to facilitate the flow of positive energy. Through breathing and other yogic exercises one becomes conscious of harmony with an ultimate unity and experiences an all-embracing Love.[140] Awakening to this spiritual experience can be visualized as a lotus flower, which, even if planted in dirty water, awakens petal by petal to a pure beauty.[141]

True spirituality need not be supernatural, but it also is not worldly. It is not centered on the cravings of the ego, but on the yearning of the spirit. Spiritual people aspire to a world that is magnificent, beautiful, and peaceful for all. These aspirations often lead them to commit themselves to working for such a world. Omid Safi, Professor of Asian and Middle Eastern Studies at Duke University elaborates: "As Confucius reminded us a long time ago," he writes, "virtue begins in the heart, and it ripples outward and outward, to transform the family, community, and the world."[142]

All of us can nurture our own spirits by attending to our values, while some people have the opportunity to work on a large scale to better the world. Some are in a position to work for causes that are committed to spiritual values like compassion and caring, justice, tolerance, respect for the environment, education for all, and the pursuit of knowledge and wisdom.

Leaders, particularly, have tremendous power when it comes to modeling and embracing spiritual values. Spiritual growth in individuals and societies can be greatly enhanced when we have leaders who exhibit empathy and moral character.

Safi points out spiritual leaders are often political leaders as well, insofar as they speak out for social justice. The renowned twentieth century writer and Trappist monk Thomas Merton was being political when he spoke out for social justice, says Safi: "His deep attachment to the life of the spirit, even silence, did not prevent him from getting involved in issues of justice and injustice, or speaking out against racism and war."[143] The same could be said, of course, for the Rev. Martin Luther King and Mahatma Gandhi, and many other spiritual leaders. Of Gandhi, it has been said that he had "no trouble bringing his spirituality and politics together."[144]

Likewise, political leaders have an opportunity to bring spirituality to their leadership—"to leave ego and power trips at the door and truly serve the good of others."[145] Decent people always yearn for "a spiritu-

ally-based politics guided by moral values."
As a people, we learned long ago "that peace,
order and cooperation . . . depend on guid-
ing principles of social harmony and trust."[146]
This knowledge is now in our DNA, and deep
down it satisfies our spiritual longing.

---

[129] *Twelve Steps to a Compassionate Life*, "Preface" (NY: Alfred A. Knopf, 2010).

[130] "Charter for Compassion," Wikipedia.

[131] "The Deepest Human Yearning," Aspen Chapel (April 28, 2103) YouTube.

[132] "Our weird universe," Robert Wright & Brian Greene, YouTube (8-17-17).

[133] "Beauty as a Compass for Truth," *onbeing.org*.

[134] Volker Kessler, "Spirituality in Mathematics," *tandfonline. com* (2019).

[135] "Robert Wright and Karen Armstrong," Meaning of Life TV, YouTube.

[136] "The Riddle of Self," *Waking Up: A Guide to Spirituality without Religion* (NY: Simon & Schuster, 2015).

[137] Quoted by Eugenia Erenchinova and Elena Proudchenko, "Spirituality and Moral Values," Abstract, *shs-conferences.org*.

[138] "Spirituality and Moral Values," 47.

[139] Joseph Campbell's final interview with Bill Moyers, PBS.

[140] "Chakra," Wikipedia.

[141] Campbell.

[142] "The Spiritual Is Political," *onbeing.org* (9 / 11 / 2016).

[143] "The Spiritual Is Political."

[144] Corrine McLoughlin, "Spiritual Politics: Innovative Approaches," *visionarylead.org* (2005).

[145] McLoughlin.

[146] Chakrabarti and Fairbanks.

Popular Spirituality

Our longing for meaning is attested to by the number of seekers of the truth who look to celebrity gurus for spiritual guidance either online, in bestselling books, or on television. A few of the most popular are Oprah Winfrey, Eckhart Tölle, and Deepak Chopra. Spirituality groups always place them near the top of lists of the most influential living spiritual leaders, right up there with the Dalai Lama and Pope Francis.[147] Oprah can be credited for putting them there in the first place because she has a wide audience to whom she recommends her favorite spiritual leaders. They become popular largely because their followers find them charismatic. At the same time, they have accumulated millions of dollars from their books and speaking engagements.

The advice offered in this popular spirituality is largely self-help. One critic characterizes Winfrey's brand as "Live your best life mumbo-jumbo, a mix of spirituality and self-help."[148] The self looms large in this New Age spirituality. It's about healing the self and empowering the self. Ross Douthat calls it "health-and-wealth spirituality."[149] While Oprah speaks of a successful life as the goal, Chopra offers to help you create "unlimited wealth with effortless ease," as well as to live practically forever through adopting his spiritual and alternative medicine practices.[150]

Tölle borrows the lessons of the Bible, but even more so the practices of Eastern religions, such as the effort to be "present." Winfrey recommends practicing gratitude by daily journaling and staying connected to a divine power. In order to be happy, they try to stay connected to a divine power that they sometimes call God, or Life Force, or Intelligence that orchestrates the energy of the universe. It is Infinite Consciousness and humans can channel it by being present and aware. Deepak Chopra speaks of it as the spiritual and creative energy of the universe. Winfrey says, " . . . let the energy of the universe lead you." Chopra claims to be applying quantum physics to this supernatural belief, but many physicists disagree with him and describe his thinking as "fuzzy." New age spirituality is sometimes called "woo-woo," and the thinking of New Age gurus has been referred to as "woolly."[151]

While the Dalai Lama, a product of long, rigorous spiritual training, wants us to be happier by thinking of others as being as important as ourselves, many celebrity gurus address primarily the need for one's own individual happiness through self-improvement. Authentic spirituality, in contrast to this self-help version, does not neglect the self, but puts the self into a larger context of humanity as a whole.

Much "fashionable spirituality," such as New Age spirituality, has led to "an almost complete self-absorption."[152] In his book *The Road to Character*, author and *New York Times* columnist David Brooks writes that since the 1960s the "self" has not been thought of as the seat of the "soul," but as a resource for worldly success. The last sixty years can be characterized as the "era of self," a self that has become narcissistic, completely autonomous, and excessively competitive. This self-interest is not a path to character.

Ross Douthat considers Elizabeth Gilbert's megaselling memoir *Eat, Love, Pray* typical of "the soul questing embraced by many liberals today."[153] (Douthat is a political and religious conservative.) While recovering from the dissolution of her first marriage, Gilbert discovered "religious ecstasy" in an ashram in India. She felt the healing power of finding the divine part of herself. Douthat calls this a narcissistic, "individualistic experience,"[154] more about feeling better than becoming deeply attuned to the meaning of life, more like therapy perhaps than spirituality.

Winfrey says that "having something to look forward to" is one of her favorite definitions of happiness. When comparing that with the Dalai Lama's prescription for happiness, that is, "being compassionate," one can decide which of the two is self-help and which is spirituality.

Norman Lear has said: "I don't know a more spiritual moment than a belly laugh."[155] Lear is only half joking; laughter has the spiritual power to connect people. There's a great deal to be said for the transcendent nature of any spiritual moment, whether it's laughter, listening to music, or viewing a sunset.

Living spiritually, however, calls for a serious transformation of behavior, not a feel-good moment. It is not easy being a spiritual person, to make one's contribution to a better world. Whenever we meet one of the criteria, however, we are on the right path. The more we do that is spiritual, the more spiritual we become. It might call for what Catholics refer to as an "examination of conscience." If one's motives are clearly within the spiritual demands of compassion, awe, and the ability to transcend selfish preoccupation, one is spiritually engaged. The more spiritually engaged one is, the more qualified one is to call oneself a spiritual person.

---

[147] See the annual lists compiled by *Watkins Magazine* of the top 100 living spiritual leaders.

[148] Brian Lowry's review of *Belief*, *chicagotribune.com* (10-19-15).

[149] "Oprah: Prophet, Priestess . . . Queen?" *NYT* (1/10/18).

[150] Wendy Kaminer, "The Spiritual is Political," *prospect.org*.

[151] "The Future of God," a debate with Chopra, Sam Harris, Michael Shermer, and Jean Houston. YouTube (October 16, 2011).

[152] Marilyn Mason, "'*Spirituality'—What on Earth Is It?*" Summer, 2000.

[153] Quoted in Mark Oppenheimer's review of Douthat's book *Bad Religion*, *NYT* (4-18-2012).

[154] "Oprah: Prophet, Priestess . . . Queen?"

[155] On CBS's "Morning Edition," December, 2020.

Nonbelievers

Atheists proclaim that there is no evidence for a God or gods. When considering the existence of a Creator and/or an afterlife, atheists believe at the very least that a supernatural cause is unlikely. Even though it is probable that scientists will never answer every question about existence, atheists believe that the physical evidence required by science offers a more satisfactory approach to tackling the mysteries of existence than does religion.

The ultimate origin of the universe remains a mystery. It would have required energy, but where did that energy come from? How did anything arise? Even as questions are answered, they give rise to new questions. The question of why there is something rather than nothing remains either unanswered or answerable.

Even the theories of theoretical physicists like Stephen Hawking and, more lately, Lawrence Krauss require something, namely, energy, to cause the Big Bang. We might never know through science why we are here.

Theists often take advantage of scientific uncertainty, such as the nature of reality at the time of the Big Bang, to suggest the probability of an interventionist God. This perspective is called the "God of the gaps." However, atheists consider it fallacious to argue that a scientific explanation being absent one can jump to a supernatural one. Moreover, as science advances, a theory such as the "God of the gaps" would inevitably weaken, as the scientist Neil deGrasse Tyson has pointed out.[156]

Hume proffered philosophical arguments that would label him a skeptic of dogmatic religious teachings. He felt that there are "alternative hypotheses that are available to us that are more plausible and consistent with human experience" than a Creator.[157] For example, he cites "the old Epicurean hypothesis of eternal matter that generates cycles of chaos and order." Hume's belief was a "non-dogmatic form of atheism."

Moreover, when we come to a conception of God, Hume suggests in his work that "the abundant evidence of unnecessary evil in the world provides us with compelling grounds for denying that there exists an omnipotent, morally perfect being who is the creator and governor of this world."[158]

Most atheists, however, count on science to reveal the true nature of reality, while knowing that absolute truth about nature is likely unattainable. Scientists compile models of how the universe works and eventually come to a consensus, which they take as empirical truth.[159] Atheists place their faith in the strong evidence that leads to scientific consensus.

Stephen Jay Gould defined "fact" in science as data, which lead to conclusions "not known with absolute certainty but 'confirmed to such a degree that it would be perverse to withhold provisional assent.'" Darwin's research, for example, presented "so many pieces of evidence" that no other configuration other than his theory could explain the facts discovered in support of evolution.[160]

While the Big Bang theory is generally accepted as having initiated the universe, questions persist about conditions before the cataclysmic event. Further results of scientific research will have far-reaching implications for humans to ponder.

Another challenging mystery for scientists is the so-called "hard problem of consciousness"— how and why humans developed an interior life whereby we became aware of our internal and external existence. Scientists have not found in the material world the source of the features that we identify as the result of consciousness, such as our ability to reason, or to do math, or to describe what we observe, or to appreciate beauty. Atheists who subscribe to scientific materialism or physicalism need to find some natural cause to account for consciousness. Neuroscientists and physicists are working on the puzzle by studying the brain.

Nor do we know, of course, if consciousness survives death in any meaningful way. Is consciousness the human soul being tested in preparation for a future life as religions would purport? Or will neuroscientists be able to locate the material source of conscious awareness? Is consciousness the sign of a creative Intelligence, not a supernatural Designer, but some natural builder of purpose in the universe, as some evolutionary biologists have theorized.[161] Others, relatively few in number, wonder if the universe is a simulation algorithm.

A few years after 9/11/2001, books promoting atheism began to appear on the bestseller lists. One of the first is titled *The End of Faith* written by Sam Harris. In it Harris blames the teachings of Islam for having inspired the al-Qaeda terrorists who directed airplanes into the World Trade Center and the Pentagon on that horrific day. Harris was soon joined by other prominent non-believing intellectuals who think of religion, particularly fundamentalist religion, as irrational. They were dubbed the "New Atheists." Four of the most prominent include Harris, Richard Dawkins, Daniel Dennett, and the late Christopher Hitchens. Three of them are eminent scientists; Hitchens was a renowned journalist. Their books are well written and are persuasive to many, but certainly not all. Rebuttals range from accusations of overconfidence in what science can account for to arrogance in denying anything positive about religion.

Agnostics: Some intellectuals, on the other hand, take a more humble approach than atheists do to the ultimate mysteries. Those who profess that they cannot believe what we do not have evidence for, whether it be the immortality of the "soul," the existence of a God or deities, or the non-existence of such, call themselves agnostics. Agnostics reject metaphysical certitude.[162] They adopt intellectual humility.

Although the idea implicit in agnosticism is ancient, it was Thomas Huxley, a colleague and advocate of Charles Darwin, who first publicly coined the term "agnostic" in 1869. He was a biologist and writer who argued for reason and evidence, rejecting belief in revelation, which the Abrahamic religions depend upon. Darwin, too, proclaimed himself an agnostic. "Huxley's principle says that it is wrong to say that one knows or believes that a proposition is true without logically satisfactory evidence." He believed that "we ought to suspend judgment on the issue of whether or not there is a God."[163]

Not all thinkers today who refer to themselves as agnostics are referring only to lack of evidence for a God or deities. Robert Wright, for example, who has called himself a spiritual agnostic, is unwilling to rule out some as yet unknown purpose or "intelligence" behind the evolution of the world. Wright's worldview does not allow for a supernatural intelligence.

[156] "2014 Neil deGrasse Tyson Interview on Bill Moyers," YouTube.

[157] *plato.stanford.edu,* "Hume on Religion."

[158] "Hume on Religion."

[159] Allison Terbush, "Truth in Science," *berkeleysciencereview.com.*

[160] "Evolution as fact and theory," Wikipedia.

[161] Robert Wright, "The New Agnosticism," YouTube.

[162] "Free Will, Determinism, and Compatiblism," Robert Wright & Gideon Rosen, YouTube.

[163] "Atheism and agnosticism," *plato.stanford.edu.*

Secular Humanism

Another philosophical worldview that has roots in centuries past and has been adopted today by millions of people worldwide is Secular Humanism. Secular Humanists think of God as "a creation of humankind itself, . . . not a divine truth transcending reason," as Christians do.[164] Therefore, Secular Humanists are atheists or sometimes agnostics.

Secular Humanism's focus is on humanity's welfare. Its stance is ethical but nonreligious, and freethinking, not doctrinal. By studying philosophy, literature, science, art, politics, psychology, and rhetoric, Humanists seek to discover what kind of society best meets mankind's needs. They are inspired, as Humanists always have been, by the Greek and Roman classics. Humanists discover the meaning of the "good life" by observing humanity, in adherence with the classical thought of Socrates, the Greek philosopher who proposed that the "considered" life is the only life worth living.[165]

It was Christian scholars during the European Renaissance who rediscovered classical thought. In addition to their theological beliefs, they promoted the Humanistic philosophy of life with its emphasis on human welfare. Christian Humanists such as Erasmus criticized the legalistic approach with which medieval Scholastic philosophers like St. Thomas Aquinas approached faith. Renaissance Humanists desired a more emotive religion. The poet Petrarch, for example, had argued that theology is effective not because it proves anything, but because it reaches the heart.[166]

Today's Secular Humanists focus on what human beings experience and hope for. While they do not believe in God, they do have faith —faith in humanity. Secular humanists celebrate reason and embrace a secular ethics. They believe that it is the relationship between people that gives life meaning, not a connection to divinity. They believe that happiness is achieved by leading a virtuous life and that God is not necessary to living a moral life. Indeed, belief in God could preclude "happiness" because they believe that "to be happy is to be secular."[167] The symbol associated with Secular Humanist organizations throughout the globe is "the happy human." The logo is imprinted with the words "Good without God."

Humanists have always valued deep learning in a wide range of subjects with a goal of "widespread civic and cultural renewal." The fourteenth century Italian poet Dante is best known for his long narrative poem *The Divine Comedy*, but he also wrote a political tract that would become "the doctrine of the separation of church and state." Later, Thomas Jefferson would credit the works of Aristotle and Cicero with teaching him to value the dignity of human beings, as had Montaigne and Erasmus before him. Jefferson, in fact, named these classical writers as sources for the Declaration of Independence.[168]

Humanists feel that learning and contemplation should lead to action. Present-day Humanist organizations are heavily committed to activism. One of the principles in the Humanist Manifesto is that "working to benefit society maximizes individual happiness." The American Humanist Association (AHA) has 250 local affiliates who engage in progressive social activism. Since 1941, their goal has been to employ reason, compassion, science, and justice in campaigns for equality and freedom of thought. AHA was one of the founding members of Humanists International, the umbrella organization, established in 1952 and is now "made up of more than 160 secular humanist, atheist, rationalist, skeptic, free thought, and Ethical Culture organizations from over 80 countries."[169]

A number of prominent persons have "proudly associated with the AHA," including Isaac Asimov, Margaret Atwood, Kurt Vonnegut, Joyce Carol Oates, Steve Wozniak,

Gloria Steinem, Steven Pinker, Jonas Salk, John Dewey, Norman Lear, and Stephen J. Gould.[170]

Philip Kitcher, a prominent British philosopher who teaches at Columbia University, lectures widely on Secular Humanism. "Secular Humanism acknowledges the bare possibility of the Transcendent, but regards the present assertion of its existence as entirely unwarranted."[171] A self-proclaimed agnostic, Kitcher points out that belief can lead to unethical action and that Secular Humanists, while decrying doctrine, insist that belief must at least be subject to ethics.

Interestingly, Kitcher recommends a "purified" or "refined" religion, one that recognizes an emotional, but not supernatural, apprehension of reality, similar to what Emerson believed was valuable for humanity. Emerson believed in an intuitive knowledge of a spiritual world. Such a religion would seek to accomplish what religions have always meant to do, that is, orient

the faithful in valuable ways, including the pro-
motion of reverence, awe, and wonder through
ritual and ceremony. Experiencing beauty, he
says, one can feel that this is how life should be.
It would make use of religious myths and stories, as long as they were understood metaphorically. It would engage in conversation with
science and the best forms of religion, like progressive Christianity, while retaining its secular
stance. In recognizing the urgency of improving
the problems of ordinary people around us,
including those of the environment, a "refined
religion" could lead to moral progress.

---

[164] Joseph Frank, *Dostoevsky: The Miraculous Years 1867-71*
(Princeton, NJ: Princeton University, 1995) 471.
[165] A.C. Grayling, *"The Origins and Future of Humanism,"*
YouTube, April 16, 2017.
[166] *The Case for God,* 167.
[167] Matthew Engelke, "Good without God," Abstract, *www. journals.uchicago.edu.*
[168] Humanism, "Early history," *brittanica.com.*
[169] "Humanists International," *en.m.Wikipedia.org.*
[170] "Famous Humanists in History," *americanhumanist.org.*
[171] "Secular Humanism: Beyond Doubt," YouTube.

Stoicism

Since the late twentieth century, there has been a resurgence of interest in the ancient philosophy of life known as Stoicism. Just as with other inherited traditions, such as Buddhism and Humanism, Stoics often pay little attention to any underlying metaphysical beliefs. Although Stoicism is not incompatible with Christianity and Judaism and over the centuries has often been adopted along with faith as a source of spiritual well-being, modern Stoicism is a secular religion. Contemporary Stoics include many atheists and agnostics among their adherents.

The views of its founders and early practitioners in Ancient Greece and Rome, however, are pertinent to modern Stoics. The ancients believed that Nature included a Force, a dynamic entity known as "eternal reason."[172] In their metaphysics, the name for this active part of nature is *Logos*. In the view of ancient Stoics, *Logos* provided design and purpose to the universe. It might be compared to Spinoza's God or Einstein's God, that is, the laws of Nature. It is something more than material, something less than supernatural. Christians would later add the supernatural and identify *Logos* as the revealed Word of God, but for the Stoics it was "natural," or what they referred to as "corporeal," albeit more than simply atoms in that, for them, this force of reason is separated from matter. It is identified as *pneuma* or "breath." In accord with this ancient conception of an ordered universe, modern Stoicism derives one of its basic principles, that is, that a good life depends on a person's ability to make good decisions based on reasoning.

The ancient Stoics believed that the world was designed to be a "vast, functional whole."[173] They viewed it as ultimately benign and purposeful. The contemporary secular Stoic view is that the laws of nature are neutral, neither benign nor malevolent.

The ancient Stoics also believed that free will and determinism are not mutually exclusive, a Compatibilist view, still current among many philosophers. Compatibilists believe that the universe is determined, but that volition is available to humans. In response to inevitable events, we are free to "act according to nature," that is, wisely—by way of reason, or, on the other hand, irrationally, that is, not "according to nature." What one does causes the future, not luck or chance. This means that we are accountable for our actions. Stoics say that "what comes about through fate comes about through you. . . . The fact that it is always within our power to withhold assent means that if we are sufficiently disciplined, we are capable of avoiding error."[174] This view differs from "crude fatalism," which suggests that the future is "fixed."

While modern Stoics might or might not believe in a designed universe with a divine, benign purpose, or with the view that free will and determinism are compatible, they nonetheless find the philosophy beneficial. Secular modern Stoics are primarily concerned with behavior that leads them to what Aristotle had called *eudaimonia*, also spelled *eudaemonia*, "a flourishing life." On the pathway to a good life, there is a wealth of practical wisdom in the ancient literature, particularly its emphasis on rational thinking.

There are two requirements to becoming a Stoic: Firstly, Stoics accept what they call "The Dichotomy of Control." Discovering that some things are under our control and some things are not is fundamental to Stoic philosophy. Stoicism recommends that we worry only about what we can control and that we adopt an attitude of indifference to what we cannot. We cannot, for example, change the past or know the future and therefore should focus on the present. There's nothing we can do about what we don't control. Reinhold Niebuhr, a Christian, greatly admired the dignity of Stoics; in fact, it was he who is credited with having composed in the 1940s the empowering prayer known as the Serenity Prayer, which embraces this Stoic premise. The prayer reads as follows:

"God, give us grace to accept with serenity the things that cannot be changed, courage to change the things that should be changed, and wisdom to distinguish the one from the other."

Some things are up to us, such as our values, our judgments, and our behavior. Stoics attempt to be indifferent to the achievement of other goals because they are not entirely under our control. Even when trying our best, we may not reach the goals we desire. It is best not to long for them. It helps also to be prepared to lose what we have. We would all like to think that we will enjoy endless good health, wealth, prestige; however, these are not guaranteed. What we can control is our attitude towards them, the appreciation of the good fortune we experience when we have it, the acceptance of misfortune as an inevitable part of living, and the recognition that our peace of mind is tied to how we react to good and bad events. We are able to control our reactions, not the outcomes, of even our best intentions. The goal of Stoicism is equanimity under every circumstance.

Everyone experiences setbacks. Stoics respond calmly to misfortunes that are not under their control. While not denying that a deep emotional response is a natural instinct and is to be expected, Stoics strive to get a handle on emotions that can become unhealthy. Instead of complaining, Stoics will practice the rational emotional response of self-compassion, recognizing that we are all vulnerable. Instead of regrets about past events, Stoics, being rational, choose to live in the present. They believe that we should lose ourselves in the flow of the present moment; appreciate what we have; and whatever the circumstances, savor the good in our lives. They would consider it wise to concentrate on the here and now; to learn from the past, but not repeat it; and to plan for the future, but not fret about it.[175]

The second requirement for calling oneself a Stoic is acceptance of the belief that practicing Stoic virtues will make one a better person. The Ancient Greek word for what the Stoics meant by "virtue" is *arete* meaning "excellence of character." The four fundamental "virtues" of Stoicism, which are required in order to excel as a person, are Wisdom, Courage, Justice, and Moderation (Temperance). There are minor virtues, like patience, but these are the big four.

Wisdom is "the ability to navigate solutions in the best possible way that is available." It is "right judgment." Through reason Stoics aim to discern what is good for their own moral character or what is not. Self-reflection, evaluating one's values, even one's aptitude, is paramount to accomplishing right judgment. "Wisdom is subdivided into good sense, good calculation, quick-wittedness, discretion, and resourcefulness."[176]

Courage, especially moral courage, is standing up and doing the right thing because action, too, is important to Stoics. "Courage is subdivided into endurance, confidence, high-mindedness, cheerfulness, and industriousness."[177]

Justice, especially social action, is doing what is right for yourself and other people— caring. "Justice is subdivided into piety, honesty, equity, and fair dealing."[178]

Moderation is doing things in the right measure.

Let it be said, at this point, that there are no "Sages" among Stoics; that is, no one is expected to be perfect. As the distinguished classical scholar Anthony (Tony) A. Long said in a speech to the 2018 Stoicon conference, the ancient Stoic writers do not "presume that any of their readers could be close to becoming a Sage, a perfectly Stoic person. Ancient Stoicism was a philosophy of progress, leading each individual to try to make the best of themselves [*sic*] according to their own personalities, attitudes, and real life situations."[179] For Stoics it is enough to try each day to be the best person that you can be.

Two recently prominent figures who apparently benefited from practicing Stoicism were Nelson Mandela, President of South Africa from 1994 to 1999, and Vice Admiral James

Stockdale, USN, both of whom courageously endured many years of imprisonment, Mandela as a political prisoner and Stockdale as a prisoner of war. Mandela was inspired to write his book *Conversation with Myself* by Marcus Aurelius's *Meditations*, which it is said he read in prison.[180] Stockdale's reflections on Stoicism have been published in two parts: *The Stoic Warrior's Triad* and *Master of My Fate.* Not long before his imprisonment he had memorized Epictetus' *Handbook.*

In 2017, the writer and software engineer Susan Fowler wrote on her blog about the pervasive culture of sexual harassment at Uber, the company where she was working. Her post eventually led to the ouster of her boss, the company's founder and CEO. She was a practicing Stoic and credits Stoicism with giving her the moral courage to take on a corrupt culture in Silicon Valley. As one commentator put it: "To her endless credit, Fowler resisted the temptation to suppress her outrage at the behaviour [*sic*] she witnessed at Uber. Her Stoicism proved deeper and more moral than conventional self-improvement."[181] Fowler, whose favorite authors include the likes of Proust and Dostoyevsky, believes that Seneca's essay "On the Shortness of Life" is "the greatest thing that has ever been written."[182]

Many people have found that Stoicism helps them to be self-disciplined. An accusation that has often been hurled at Stoics, however, is that they are "men of stone."[183] It is said that they mean for us to extinguish our feelings. The philosopher William B. Irvine, author of *A Guide to the Good Life*, defends Stoicism on this point. It is negative emotions, like fear, anger, and grief, he says, that Stoics wish to minimize in our lives and in so doing, leave room for us to experience joy. While we use the word "stoical," with a lowercase "s," to mean indifference to suffering or austere calm, Irvine points out, the true goal of Stoicism as a philosophy of life is directed at experiencing tranquility and joy.

Stoics allow themselves "the good feelings," namely "joy, watchfulness, and wishing." Under "wishing" they include "kindness, generosity, and warmth," emotions that are "well-reasoned and not excessive."[184]

The cognitive psychologist and practitioner of Stoicism Donald Robertson cites Marcus Aurelius on the various sources of joy for the Stoic. The first is "Contemplating virtue in ourselves." Marcus describes this as the primary source of both 'serenity' and 'joy' for the Stoic Sage. The second is "Contemplating virtue in others." Reflecting on the good qualities of those close to one, such as their modesty and generosity, will "gladden" one's heart. The third source of joy is gratitude for what one already has, while contemplating how much it would be missed if not there.[185]

Nevertheless, scholars like the philosopher Martha Nussbaum and the social psychologist Jonathan Haidt have written of the need for contemporary Stoics to correct the classical view of the emotions. For example, in his letters, Seneca, the Roman emperor and prominent ancient Stoic, counsels against feeling excessive grief. He would have grieving persons attempt to reason with themselves. They could ask themselves whether the grief they feel is what their deceased loved ones would want for them. Nussbaum, on the other hand, points out that grief is a normal instinct when one suffers the loss of someone deeply loved. She rejects the "Stoic position that passion-based choices are necessarily irrational."[186] Nussbaum believes that Stoics take it too far when they say that only our judicious response to events matters and that we should lose love of children, family, and other "externals."[187] According to Nussbaum, "Understanding our emotions helps us build a morally just society and relate to one another in a way that is deeply respectful and moral."[188]

While she believes that the Stoics are on the right track when counseling adherents to wean themselves from too great an attachment to worldly success and goods, Nussbaum thinks that they need to develop an appreciation for the significance of emotions in their philosophy of life.

Haidt would agree that contemporary thinkers need to revisit the ancient Greek and Roman attitude towards emotional attachment to "people, goals, and pleasure." The classical Stoics recommend non-attachment to "external goods and non-striving for them, but fail to see that passionate attachment can also result in joy. The life they recommend, that is, one of "cerebral reflection and emotional indifference," are lives "designed to avoid passion, and a life without passion is not a human life."[189] Haidt cites the Romantic writers on the joys of passionate experience, such as Thoreau's ecstatic appreciation of nature.

Haidt wishes us to recognize that "Happiness comes from within, and happiness comes from without." In reflecting on the ancients, as well as on modern positive psychology, he comes to the conclusion that "happiness" stems from the relationship between the internal and the external aspects of life. Humans, he says, need love, work, and a connection to something larger, in addition to wisdom, to lead a meaningful life.[190] The most satisfying life, according to Haidt, is one of "vital engagement."[191] And that involves not only coping mechanisms, such as Stoicism can provide, but also externals, such as a healthy living/working environment, rewards, and a coherence between one's strengths and one's responsibilities. Happiness can even result from striving and "passionate attachment" if the goals and accomplishments are worthy ones. "We just need some balance . . . and some specific guidance . . . about what to strive for."[192]

In her book *Stoic Wisdom*, Nancy Sherman, a classics scholar and a distinguished

professor, offers a close textually based pre-
sentation of ancient Stoicism and a correction
to misinterpretations of the philosophy. While
she would agree that contemporary philosophers and psychologists have a great deal to
offer in reconsidering the ancients, including
their views on the emotions, she contends
that the ancient Stoics do play a role in that
they actually developed a highly sophisticat-
ed description of the emotions and how to
manage them. They saw, for example, that
the emotions are multi-layered, that we have
"autonomic arousal," which can "outstrip reason." These impulses attach to what we pre-
fer, not to what's good or bad. Although they
are difficult to reign in, we must work to "nip
them in the bud," especially when it comes
to fear and anger, two of the emotions upon
which the Stoics dwelled. The second tier of
emotions are the ordinary ones we experience
every day, which need to be conditioned to
support the overall goal of the Stoics, that is,
to have our emotions service the moral good.

By cultivating the emotions according to Stoic thought practices, our emotions reach the final level that encourages moral behavior. When we have cultivated our emotions according to Stoic techniques and practices, we possess the final tier of the emotions, that is, the rational emotions that are in everyone's best interest. Sherman, who also has extensive training in psychoanalysis, has observed that the ancient Stoics uncovered the strong cognitive component of emotions that are recognized by today's psychologists. It is our job, they believed, to appraise the events in the world judiciously and to give or withhold our assent to them.

Sherman writes to dispel some of the other misconceptions and misinterpretations of the ancients that some modern Stoics believe. For example, the notion of facing life without emotion, with "a stiff upper lip." On the contrary, she says, the Stoics were all about cultivating emotion, not doing away with

it. Professor Sherman was invited to the US
Naval Academy to fill the inaugural Chair in
Ethics following the massive cheating scan-
dal that plagued the school. While there she
encountered among her students the notion
that the vicissitudes of life must be faced with
"grit" alone, what she says many lauded as
"sucking it up and moving on." Sherman
witnessed much suffering among veterans
and even "boot camp" survivors through an
unwillingness to believe in self-compassion.
The ancient Stoics would have considered it
unwise to foster an unhealthy emotion such as
grit at all costs, and to not admit one's vulner-
ability. They were not about "going it alone."
One ought not to be reluctant to seek help.
Moreover, one does not grow from "grit," she
says. "Adversity is not a blessing."[193]

Another criticism leveled at Stoicism is
its seeming inattention to social activism, for
encouraging the passive acceptance of one's
fate. For example, Ada Palmer, a professor of

history at the University of Chicago, wishes that the philosophy would teach us how
to change some of the "terrible aspects of
the world," rather than simply adapting to
them.[194] Palmer believes that Stoicism offers
"invaluable advice for taking better care of
ourselves inside," but needs to be mixed with
"other ideas" to overcome "a big blind spot
regarding the world outside ourselves, and
whether we should change it."[195]

A similar charge is brought by the Classics
professor Emily Wilson (University of
Pennsylvania) in her biography of the Stoic
philosopher Seneca. Interestingly, both she
and Palmer refer specifically to Seneca, who as
Emperor of the Roman Empire presumably was
in a position to influence the society he ruled.
"Seneca's Stoic insistence that the real Empire
exists in the mind—the real slavery is slavery
to the passions," says Wilson, might have "enabled him to deny the real corruption involved
in the real empire, with real slavery."[196]

However, its defenders point out that one of Stoicism's foundational precepts is "Justice," caring about the welfare of all living creatures.[197]

Ancient philosophers viewed human beings as socially connected with the world. Many called themselves "citizens of the world." Their view was cosmopolitan. It was ultimately essential to care about not only one's own family, but to empathize with inhabitants of the circle farthest from one's own. Many of today's modern practitioners of Stoicism make it an "all about me" self-improvement practice, but the ancients made it about healing the world.[198]

We should remember that Stoicism asks us to use our reason to live according to nature. By nature, Stoics believe, we are social animals, meaning that we are interconnected and therefore it is incumbent upon us to take care of one another. Building a better society would benefit all. The reader will find frequent references to the Stoic principle of kinship to all mankind and to nature as a whole in the works of Marcus Aurelius.[199]

One of the main goals of the ancient Stoics was "to equip the agent to be socially effective by freeing him or her from debilitating and harmful emotions," according to Anthony Long. Long interprets this understanding of social utility as equivalent to that of such humanitarian organizations as "Doctors without Borders, UNICEF, and Human Rights Watch."[200] In fact, Stoic doctrine, he says, would have the wise man be active, not resigned, certainly not self-absorbed. "We have to figure out the specific role that we can play best and beautifully, but no ancient Stoic would want to be a solitary or a hermit."[201]

Some practitioners of modern secular Stoicism, such as Tim Ferriss and Ryan Holiday, sometimes exhibit "a narrow and misleading" reading of the Stoics.[202] It is not true, for example, that the Stoics thought that we should love and accept our fate. Instead, they gave us techniques for correcting our biases. By changing the way we perceive the world, we could change the world and even our "fate."[203]

Classics scholars would have modern practitioners take a deeper look at the original texts, such as the letters of Seneca, the meditations of Marcus Aurelius, and the teachings of Epictetus, to find greater substance than can be found among some contemporary podcasters and entrepreneurs from Silicon Valley. Among those who were deeply familiar with the ancient Stoics were the founders of Cognitive Behavioral Therapy, a highly recommended form of psychotherapy, which largely displaced Freudian psychoanalysis during the twentieth century. Finding that it was a source of emotional resilience building, Allen Beck and Albert Ellis adopted Stoicism as the foundation of their therapy. Both Stoicism and CBT recognize, for example, that being realistic about our beliefs and expectations will lead to a well-adjusted life.[204] While Stoicism is more than therapy, in that it is a practical, personal philosophy, both focus on changing cognitive distortions.

What the ancients gave us, were "ways in which we look at each other as building community together through reason, humanity and …psychological habits of mind … [that] get us into better places than we are now."[205] The Stoic practice of cultivating wisdom, courage, justice, and moderation leads to tranquility of mind. To quote Marcus Aurelius: "… if nothing presents itself that's superior to the spirit that lives within – the one that has subordinated individual desires to itself, that discriminates among impressions, that is broken free of physical temptations, and subordinated itself to the gods, and looks out for human beings welfare – if you find that there is nothing more important or valuable than that, then do not make room for anything but it." (*Meditations*)

---

[172] "Stoicism," *plato.stanford.edu.*

[173] Ada Palmer, "Stoicism's Appeal to the Rich and Powerful," *exurbe.com.* March 27, 2019.

[174] "Stoicism," s*tanford.plato.org.*

[175] Massimo Pigliucci "Stoicism 101," YouTube, 2015.

[176] "Stoic Ethics," *iep.utm.edu/stoiceth.*

[177] "Stoic Ethics."

[178] "Stoic Ethics."

[179] "Stoicon 2018: Tony Long 'Stoicism Ancient and Modern,'" *modernstoicism.com.*

[180] David Ulin, "Nelson Mandela, remembered through his books," *latimes.com.*

[181] Rowland Manthorpe, "All that's good and bad about Silicon Valley's Stoicism fad," *wired.com.uk,* October 10, 2017.

[182] Massimo Pigliucci, "Susan Fowler as a modern Stoic role model," *howtobeastoic.wordpress.com.*

[183] Dirk Baltzy, "Stoicism," *stanford.plato.com.*

[184] Baltzy.

[185] "Three Sources of Joy in the Stoicism of Marcus Aurelius," *donaldrobertson.com.*

[186] Aidan Johnson, "Martha Nussbaum respects the Cynic-Stoic tradition—but she's ready to correct it," a*mericamagazine.org.* November 11, 2019.

[187] Jules Evans, "An interview with Martha Nussbaum on Neo-Stoicism,"*emotionsblog.history.amulet.ac.uk*, November 22, 2012. Also see her book *Upheavals of Thought*.

[188] "Martha Nussbaum on Emotions, Ethics and Literature," *partiallyexaminedlife.com*.

[189] *The Happiness Hypothesis* (New York: Basic Books, 2006) 105.

[190] *The Happiness Hypothesis*, 238-9.

[191] *The Happiness Hypothesis*, 223.

[192] *The Happiness Hypothesis*, 106.

[193] "Nancy Sherman: *Stoic Wisdom* with Ezekiel Emanuel," P&P Live. YouTube.

[194] "Stoicism's Appeal to the Rich and Powerful," *exurbe*, March 27, 2019.

[195] "Stoicism's Appeal to the Rich and Powerful."

[196] Quoted by Roland Manthorpe, "All that's good and bad about Silicon Valley's Stoicism fad," *wired.com.uk*, 10/26/2017.

[197] Pigliucci.

[198] Pigliucci.

[199] Robertson, "Three Sources of Joy in the Stoicism of Marcus Aurelius," *donaldrobertson.com*.

[200] "Stoicisms Ancient and Modern," *modernstoicism.com*.

[201] "Stoicisms Ancient and Modern."

[202] Nancy Sherman, "Five myths about Stoicism," *The Washington Post*," June 1, 2021.

[203] Sherman, "Five myths about Stoicism."

[204] John Mathews, "Stoicism and CBT," December 6, 2015, *https://www.vacounseling.com/stoicism-cbt*.

[205] Simon J. E. Drew, "Ancient Lessons for Modern Resilience," interview with Nancy Sherman, YouTube.

Tapping into the Mystery

There are ways to live with mystery—approaches that the poet John Keats called "negative capability." Two of the most significant avenues for scientists and philosophers, as well as for anyone who is reflective, are <u>questioning</u> and <u>reverence</u>.

In a fascinating discourse between the believer Marilynne Robinson and the agnostic Marcelo Gleiser, the novelist and physicist agree that questioning and revering the unknown, are spiritual exercises. They are responses to mystery that, in fact, unite the fields of science and religion.[206]

Questions are exciting because we know there is "always more to learn," says Gleiser. Science can sometimes provide answers, as in the theory of evolution or that of the Big

Bang, which provide evidence that seems to have explained how our universe works. We will never know everything, as in Einstein's unsatisfactory attempt to find a unified theory, because we are incapable of measuring everything in this complex universe. It is thrilling, however, to find evidence to support a hypothesis in the continuously advancing exploration of our universe. Geiser points to the evidential data gathered by the Hubbell Space Telescope, which offers the "best explanation" for the Big Bang theory. The experience, he says, is like the feeling one gets when adding a piece to the jigsaw puzzle.

Another means of living with mystery is the feeling of reverence one feels towards nature. As humans we feel awe at the enormity and beauty of the universe. Gleiser says that his spirituality is his feeling of connection to nature, and that his questions are a form of worship. Robinson, as we have seen, finds intimations of truth in the beauty of nature. She identifies with the American Transcendentalists. Interestingly, both Robinson and Gleiser grew up very close to nature—Gleiser near the sea in Rio de Janiero and Robinson in the Idaho mountains.

Robinson reminds us that humans have always questioned their environment and craved answers. Ancient humans looked inward for their explanations and created myths to explain what they could not understand. They developed a religious instinct, a universal instinct that moderns have neglected. She suggests that the myths are often not far off from what scientists have eventually discovered, such as the gradual workings of evolution or that the universe had a beginning. She also points to what humans have always experienced, that is, intimations that there is something more to reality that we cannot know. Thus, we create hypotheses in order to gain some control and to keep us sane.

Both scientific and religious questions reveal how we crave knowledge, she says. We yearn to know who we are and what is expected of us in this world. Science and religion make us wonder. Uncertainty is necessary, but the mystery creates wonder. When scientists and philosophers posit hypotheses, we respond with amazement and with creative speculation.

Although he rejected religious dogma and doctrine, as well as the existence of a personal God who would reward and punish his creatures, Einstein considered himself "a deeply religious man," not an atheist or even a Pantheist. His philosophy of religion was rationalistic: he believed that "God manifests Himself 'in the laws of the universe as a spirit vastly superior to that of man, and one in the face of which we with our modest powers must feel humble.'"[207]

For Einstein, it was mystery that inspired his cosmic religious feelings. "The most beautiful experience we can have is the mysterious.

It is the fundamental emotion which stands at the cradle of true art and true science. Whoever does not know it and can no longer wonder, no longer marvel, is as good as dead, and his eyes are dimmed."[208]

The physicist Frank Wilczek considers the world a beautiful work of art—wonder and awe enough. Wilczek says that there are different ways of observing the world and that sometimes they conflict. This notion is called "complementarity"—"the idea that two different ways of regarding reality can both be true, but not at the same time."[209] Wilczek suggests that different intuitions (alternative views) must both be taken into account when seeking to understand reality. See his book *Beautiful Question*. "To do full justice to reality," he says, "we must engage it from different perspectives."[210]

Many people fear the truth. They do not want to be persuaded against what they have come to believe. The philosopher and mathematician Bertrand Russell took exception to this attitude. He said that dogmatic people go through life

> … imprisoned in the prejudices derived from common sense, from the habitual beliefs of [their] age or [their] nation, and from the convictions which have grown up in [their] mind[s] without the cooperation or consent of [their] reason. To such a [person] the world tends to become definite…and unfamiliar possibilities are contemptuously rejected. As soon as we begin to philosophize, on the contrary, we find…that even the most every day things lead to problems to which only very incomplete answers can be given. Western Philosophy…removes the somewhat arrogant dogmatism of those who have never traveled into the region of liberating doubt.[211]

Both Einstein and Darwin would agree. They were scientists who respected doubt, who had questions about the existence of

God. Einstein said he liked neither religious fanatics, nor fanatical atheists. For Darwin, the problem of evil cast doubt on his belief in God.

That the physical world is not perfect, such as would reflect a perfect God, is further cause for doubt. An eclipse of the sun, for example, is an irregularity, as is a tornado, which can be set off by changes in atmosphere. The universe is full of imbalances (Gleiser). For scientists it is anathema to say that something is absolutely true. Scientists do, however, feel what astrophysicist Natalie Batalho has called a "deep reverence for the mystery."[212]

Although she is referring to an unsolved crime, the novelist Susan Orleans effectively describes how we can be moved by mystery in general. The mystery, she writes, is "like a suspended chord in the last measure of a song—that singular, dissonant, open sound that makes you ache to hear something more."[213]

In response to the mystery and magnificence of the Cosmos, science and religion share the spiritual sense of awe. While scientists continually pursue objective evidence to back up their hypotheses and religions mostly rely on faith, they both experience the thrill of seeking and the joy of reverence.

[206] "The Mystery We Are," *onbeing.org*, 11/21/19.

[207] Quoted in Max Jammer, *Einstein and Religion*, a Princeton University e-book, *academia.edu*, 144.

[208] *Einstein and Religion*, 73.

[209] Maria Popova, "Nobel-Winning Physicist Frank Wilczek on Complementarity ...." *themarginalian.org*.

[210] *onbeing.org*. 6-17-17.

[211] *The Problems of Philosophy*.

[212] "Cosmic Imagining, Civic Pondering," Popova and Natalie Batalha, *onbeing.org*, March 29, 2018.

[213] *The Library Book* (New York: Simon & Schuster, 2018) 309.

Committing to a Way of Life

Throughout history humans have felt conscious of something spiritual in themselves, something beyond day-to-day material existence. While we cannot answer with certitude the question, "Why are we here?" we can choose our thoughts, our values, and a helpful way of life. We can construct a meaningful existence.

On what do we rely when in anguish or desperation? Not on our worldly possessions, but on our transcendent convictions. We learn to accept what we cannot control, whether it be the mysterious ways of our God or the realities of the natural world, including death. Either way we want to live the best life we can. A worldview can ground us. It is a foundation for our commitments. We have a better idea of why we are committing to a lifestyle.

A philosophy of life includes an opinion about God. Some believe that a personal God exists, accessible by way of Scripture or by human instinct. Others believe only in Nature and what scientific evidence provides us. Since every concept of the nature of the universe, of the why or how it exists, encounters mystery, one's beliefs must be recognized as uncertain. We live in a state of *unknowing*, but we can choose to live well in it.

If the value of living more spiritually is clear to us and we commit to it, there are numerous habits and practices, both private and public, that will nurture that commitment. The purpose of practicing spirituality is to care for one's spirit, as we care for our bodies, by taking care of our thoughts, and feelings, and actions. They run the gamut from acts of kindness and character-building to activism. Our personalities and opportunities and where we fall on the spiritual spectrum will all determine how we proceed.

Cooperating with and caring for one another might be designed into us, but it is we who must decide to cultivate our spirituality, to become more self-giving. Maria Popova calls the nurturing "enlarging our souls." She conceives of one's soul not as a supernatural entity, but as one's personhood. It's "impossible to be a decent person without tending to it the way you would tend to a garden."[214]

As we have seen, compassion for others is intrinsic to spirituality. We might begin there. "You won't get transcendence unless you are compassionate,"says Karen Armstrong, founder of the Charter for Compassion. Loving one's neighbor is not so much a feeling or sentiment as it is a commitment. We are "a cosmic accident," says Popova. If chance has dealt us a good hand, we have a special responsibility to expand chance for everyone else. "That's all we can do. That's the most we can do."[215]

Nurturing our compassion and thereby our commitment to others is fostered by empathy, that is, understanding how another feels. Opening up to the pain of others is a spiritual activity. It can lead to acts of kindness, to altruism, and even to political conflict resolution.[216] It is important, however, to develop the right kind of empathy. Putting oneself in another person's shoes might lead to debilitating stress or even to unfairly siding with one's own group. On the other hand, striving for a cognitive empathy, which imagines another person's perspective, will better precipitate an emotional response on one's own part and lead to positive action. It is not necessary to *feel* the other person's pain; it is adequate simply *knowing* what the other person feels, that is, exercising moral imagination.

We nurture our propensity for compassion by way of commitment, habit, discipline, and practice. One of the most helpful habits to cultivate is curiosity, that is, asking questions of other people and listening closely to their responses. Another is exposing oneself to people of different cultures and races and perspectives by way of movies and novels. In one's own social interactions with people, one can look for similarities instead of differences. Everyone has what have been called "empathy blocks... areas where you feel it's hard to connect to people and relate to their experiences." Noticing these patterns and focusing on them can help to override them.[217]

An age-old contemplative practice called "mindfulness" is another practice that can facilitate caring and other spiritual goals. It employs methods "designed to quiet . . . the mind, to cultivate a capacity for deepened awareness, concentration, and insight." It teaches one how to cleanse one's mind of its propensity to be habitually chattering, judging oneself and others, as well as how to offset the distractions of multitasking.[218] Practicing mindfulness takes us more deeply into reality and cultivates the spiritual experience of wonder. Practitioners "realize with astonishment what rewards they reap when they pay greater attention to their moment-by-moment experience of life."[219]

One can also achieve a contemplative mindset by writing, by listening to music, by "beholding" art, by studying and learning, or by reading serious literature. When we participate in these practices, we are seeking insight. Reading Theodore Dostoyevsky's *Brothers Karamazov*, for example, gives us insight into the lives of characters experiencing religious faith and religious angst, and we grasp the truth that metaphysical questioning is universal. Literature is the study of life. Insight is likewise gained through art and music. When a painter paints an object or a composer creates a song, a whole world opens up. We can absorb the creative artist's illumination of reality, even gain intimacy with it, by giving it mindful attention.[220]

These contemplative practices become spiritual experiences. One scientific study has discovered a specific gene that can be associated with spiritual-mystical experience and perhaps a predisposition to faith, if not to any specific belief system.[221] It is an endorphin-producing gene. Buddhists would describe this spiritual propensity somewhat poetically, as a disposition that helps to "establish a general trust in the universe, a sense of openness and generosity."[222] Practices of meditation and yoga can facilitate such experience.

Evolutionary psychologists theorize that we are also hardwired for religion, that as a species we have developed an instinct for religious behavior, including sharing rituals within our group and finding supernatural agency for things we don't understand. For our earliest ancestors, feelings of empathy and cooperation, as well as moral behavior, became intuitive. When humanity's numbers began to grow, the need for social cohesion also became significant. Large numbers of people were living together in close proximity. Religious experience, which was "doctrine-less" at this time, became an endorphin-producing experience enabled by music, by a ritual dance or trance, and even by laughter.[223] It enabled "social equilibrium."

Later in human history, churches became an outlet for community gathering. They offered not only the opportunity for connection to a God, but also for cooperation within a group and therefore survival. Many today still benefit from spiritual opportunities found in congregations. As of 2021, however, "less than half of all Americans claim membership in a house of worship (specifically churches, synagogues or mosques").[224] Many are rejecting dogma and doctrine and looking for alternative group activity in order to connect to the transcendent and to the world. They call themselves "spiritual but not religious."

Some SBNRs participate in huge events like Burning Man, an annual celebration held in Black Rock Desert, NV, and other sites around the globe. The tone of Burning Man is one of radical creativity. It is an artistic community where everyone is expected to participate "in balancing cooperation, self-reliance, individual expression, and creative collaboration."[225] While they do have critics (attendance is mostly White, ticket prices are high, sometimes they leave a large carbon footprint and huge amounts of trash), the principles set forth by the founder are spiritually sound. Attendants seek to experience the transcendent in the ordinary experiences of life – – through nature, art, and music and through the giving and receiving of gifts. They seek to achieve diversity and inclusiveness. Their emphasis is on universal love rather than on man's sinfulness or depravity. They feel more spiritual and able to express themselves and their intuitions in a non-judgmental, non-proselytizing manner than they did in traditional religions. As their congregations dwindle, church communities are watching and attempting to learn how to reach out to the SBNRs.

Whether we find spiritual connection to others through mindfulness or in group activities or both, underlying our spiritual strength is our moral behavior. Most of us know some of the rules of conduct that were developed by the world's religions, such as "Do unto others, as you would have others do unto you" (Confucius and Jesus). A sense of right and wrong has been built into our genes and can function unless that sense is damaged by a morally stressful upbringing. The trick is to think clearly about our goals and align our behavior with what we know is moral or ethical.

Whether we act in an ethical way because it is the right thing to do (Kant) or because "virtuous" behavior will make us happier (Aristotle), with practice, habits of salutary behavior can become ingrained. We can even overcome behavior that is harmful to ourselves and others, as we know from addiction programs.

The development of good habits is what makes for a good character. To become ingrained, habits need to be practiced. Practicing moral habits begins with naming the habits we wish to develop. Some prominent ones are honesty, moral courage, compassion, generosity, fidelity, integrity, fairness, self-control, and good judgment. These are not personality traits, traits which are innate; on the contrary, character traits are based on beliefs, for example, that honesty or treating others well is important.[226] Character traits can, albeit with great effort, be changed over time. To move towards the ideals of character, one engages in moral behavior until it becomes one's automatic dispositional state.

Morality is by its nature communal. We live in communities and our morals develop over time in an effort to foster cooperation. Humans have developed a moral core, and it is apparently not relative to the societies in which we live as has been thought. Anthropologists at the University of Oxford have studied sixty societies from around the world and discovered seven universal moral rules.[227] They are as follows: "help your family, help your group, return favours [*sic*], be brave [have moral courage], defer to superiors, divide resources fairly, and respect others' property." The results show that people everywhere believe that promoting the common good is the right thing to do.

As developmental psychologists like Paul Bloom have noted, however, we tend to care more for kin than for strangers. We are less kind to strangers. The authors of the Oxford study hope that research like theirs will promote cross-cultural cooperation. All groups develop the same moral codes to survive and live harmoniously. Understanding how much we have in common ought to promote mutual understanding. That is now the challenge.

When it comes to beliefs and practices, we initially follow those of our family members, especially if they were loving and supportive. In adulthood, we might evaluate those beliefs through study and reflection, and choose a different path. We might also draw wisdom from more than one worldview. Our worldviews are perspectives, how we think about the world given what we have learned and experienced. Everyone's viewpoint needs to be allowed, but open to discussion.

Studying the ideas of various movements and religions can help us understand what we value and to what code of conduct we wish to commit. A commitment can be made to a belief and a way of life that expresses one's deepest values and feelings, that appeals to both one's mind and feelings. A determination of what one needs for spiritual gratification will lead one to a chosen way of life. Religions can make us feel good in that they allow for a Providence in our world and a Creator who has a plan.

Religions and secular spiritual movements can offer public rituals and opportunities for belonging to a community. Contemplation, however, is also salutary; and while it is private, its results play out when we interact with others in a spiritual way in everyday life.

Whatever view of reality we adopt and however we commit ourselves, it is within our power to deliberate, to practice compassion, and to live better lives. We can pray or practice mindfulness and transcend our single "selves." We can connect and cooperate, quell our egos, and face the eternal questions better prepared and spiritually enriched.

---

[214] "Cosmic Imagining, Civic Pondering."

[215] "Cosmic Imagining, Civic Pondering."

[216] Ashley Abramson, "Cultivating Empathy," *apa.org*, November 1, 2021.

[217] Abramson.

[218] Chick, N. (2010). Mindfulness in the Classroom. Vanderbilt University Center for Teaching. *https://*cft.vanderbilt.edu/guides-sub-pages/contemplative-pedagogy/.

[219] Chick, N. (2010). Citing Sid Brown, "Cultivating Wonder," *Sewanee Magazine*, Spring 2008.

[220] Chick, N. (2010). Citing Deborah Haynes, "Contemplative Practice and the Education of the Whole Person."

[221] Dean Hamer, *The God Gene*, 2004.

[222] Robert Thurman, quoted in *Philosophy of Religion, qcc.cuny. edu*, Chapter 10. Section 5.

[223] Brandon Ambrosino, "Do humans have a 'religion instinct'?" *bbc.com*, May 5, 2019. (Ambrosino quotes the evolutionary psychologist Robin Dunbar.)

[224] Mike Clawson, "Nomads & Nones," *The New Story*, May 5, 2021. Clawson cites *news.gallup.com*.

[225] "Burning Man," *brittanica.com*.

[226] Alex Lickerman, MD, "Personality vs. Character," *psychologytoday.com*, April 3, 2011.

[227] Curry, Oliver Scott, Daniel Austin Mullins and Harvey Whitehouse, "Is It Good to Cooperate?" *journals.uchicago.edu*.

Conclusion

Reflecting on the philosophical and religious hypotheses reviewed above can help readers to clarify their own views. Many will determine that the supernatural explanation for existence is probable. Others will view a supernatural reality as not probable or even reasonable and accept the view that existence is probably the result of natural forces. Learning what one thinks is called getting to know oneself.

To identify as a fundamentalist or atheist is to adopt an extreme perspective. Belief in the literal truth of the scriptures may be difficult to defend, as is denying the possibility of a God. Neither hypothesis can be proved. Believers could try a more enlightened view that interprets the events in their scriptures as metaphors. Nonbelievers could remain open minded and propose only that science has not supported a supernatural reality. Reasoning alone will not arrive at metaphysical truth. Atheists' faith in nature is as reasonable as believers' faith in God. Agnostics who believe that we cannot know, that we might never know, the nature of ultimate reality can likewise be said to hold a reasonable belief.

It would be helpful to remember that "believers" present opinions, not facts. Many persons of Faith know this and choose simply to *trust* that God exists. They do not claim certitude. By the same token, open-minded atheists proclaim not the impossibility of a God, but the lack of hard evidence to prove the existence of God.

We need to avoid certitude when forming opinions about the Cosmos. Doubt must accompany faith. Certitude can be murderous.

We can and should engage in dialogue, but it needs to be tolerant of another's beliefs and focused on what way of being is best for the world and humanity. Too much current dialogue amounts to debate on the superiority of one position over another. We are one world, with one universe to explore and one biosphere to save.[228] On that we can agree. With the coexistence of extraordinary wealth and dire poverty, as well as suffering of one kind or another by everyone, we have plenty to motivate us to try to uphold the deepest and most common remedies suggested over time by the greatest spiritual traditions. Doing so, that is, practicing compassion, generosity, respect for others, and tolerance, as recommended by Abraham, the Buddha, Jesus, and Mohammad, can constitute a meaningful life for everyone.

---

[228] Mary-Jane Rubinstein, "The Case for Cosmic Pantheism," *nautilus.us*, August 27, 2017.

Acknowledgments

A big thank you to Louise Michot for her support and expert editing; likewise, to Marianne Santo Domingo for her valuable feedback; and to Linda Kenny and Dolores Killeen for believing in me. Thank you, also, to Khalil Michot for his professional design and photography contributions.

Milton Keynes UK
Ingram Content Group UK Ltd.
UKHW012249231123
433173UK00002B/13